the gift of moments

to John & Ethan —
Trust that God is working
in every moment!
Lauren Stephens
2 Corinthians 12:9

Lauren Stephens

The Gift of Moments
Copyright © 2015 by Lauren Stephens
Cover Photographs by Lauren Stephens
All Rights Reserved

ISBN-13: 978-1514257647
ISBN-10: 1514257645

The stories in this book are based on true accounts. For privacy, all character names and some appearances, dates, and locations, have been altered, though the "moment" in each story remains entirely accurate. The author gratefully acknowledges the many friends, family, and complete strangers who willingly shared their stories of the miraculous occurrences witnessed in their lives.

THE GIFT OF MOMENTS

*For Mama,
who taught me the true value of a gift*

Table of Contents

Introduction: My Thoughts..................13

Before I Even Knew You..................21

Just Like in the Movies..................40

20,000 lbs..................60

Chloe..................79

Sticky Notes..................100

A Key and the Cross..................119

More Than Just a Goal..................142

A Different Kind of Healing..................166

The Man With the Dreads..................195

Just Go..................219

The Last Melon..................240

The Midnight Visitor..................262

Epilogue..................286

Acknowledgements..................289

My Thoughts

Psalm 73:28 – But as for me, it is good to be near God. I have made the Sovereign Lord my refuge; I will tell of all your deeds.

When I set out to write this book almost five years ago, I had no idea what it would look like or where it would take me. I felt like God had planted stories in my heart that He wanted me to tell, but I didn't know how I could come up with words that would be expressive enough to clearly show the grace of His hand and the beautiful way He strings events in our lives together for His purposes and our good - down to the very smallest detail. I didn't know where to begin.

And while I still don't think that any words I could ever share would be adequate to tell you about the greatness of our God, I have decided that He didn't call me to be a masterful writer but rather an obedient child.

The thing about obedience is that there's no prerequisite to it. You don't have to understand why you're being asked to do or not do something, but you are expected to abide by the guidelines set before you – sometimes without fully understanding. Parents don't need to provide their child with their reasons for why he should or should not do something, though often they do. The role of the child is to obey his parents out of respect and love. No questions asked.

That's what *The Gift of Moments* is about. It's an almighty God loving on His children because they in turn choose to love and obey Him, often without fully understanding. It's finding that God works in crazy fun ways even in the middle of those ordinary, mundane days. It's giving God the glory for the "coincidences" – the God Moments – that I choose to believe are His miracles, not just happenstance. That's what I had just started to discover five years ago when I set out on the journey that would become this book.

Before I share the first of these stories, I want to give you a glimpse at the heart of the twenty-year-old me who, before she even had a minute's worth of writing training, penned her thoughts that would become the thread that holds this book together. The following words are those I recorded after my return from a mission trip to Haiti. While there, living and working among the people, God impressed this book upon my heart, and in my pursuit of obedience to Him, these are the words that poured forth onto the pages of my journal.

For years, it has been the desire of my heart to author a book. And for years, I have not known what to say, much less where to begin. Struggling with thoughts of inadequacies, I could not imagine why anyone would ever want to read anything that I might say. THAT, however, is the beauty of this book. These are not my words; they are my Father's. These are not my stories; they are His. And I did not create these moments; they are all gifts, lavished by Him alone.

This past summer, I spent ten of the most amazing days of my life in the mountains of Cayes, which is a small rural village smack dab in the middle of Haiti. One of the cries of my heart as I tried to prepare for a trip of this magnitude was that I would see God. Like, really see Him.

Having grown up in church from practically the day I was born, I've heard countless stories of missionaries returning to the

States, so wowed by the ways in which God had manifested Himself to them while in a foreign country. In the days approaching my own international trip, aside from flying, my greatest fear was that I was going to miss God in Haiti. How or why exactly I thought that would happen, I honestly cannot say. I just know that I spent countless hours in prayer before the trip and that topping the list of my requests was that I would not return from Haiti to report that I had not witnessed God at work.

So from the moment I stepped off of solid ground and onto my first flight at the Atlanta airport, I knew that this trip was going to have to be all God. There was simply too much that could go wrong unless He kept it all going right. And that is when I started looking, really *looking, for His hand at work in any and every situation.*

Determined to see God above all else, I suppose it really shouldn't have surprised me that one of the first things I saw out of the window of our plane as we prepared to touch down on the Port au Prince airstrip was a cross, etched into the side of one of the tallest mountains on the island of Haiti. Technically the cross was the intersection of roads way up near the apex of the mountain. Regardless, it was one of those, "Wow, God, sometimes you are just too much" kind of moments. As it would turn out, this very same cross was also the last thing I remember seeing as I left Haiti a mere ten days later.

The Sunday after our arrival back home, my mission team was sharing with the church youth group some of the stories and experiences from our incredible journey, and of all things, I decided to share with them about this very fear. It was in that upstairs room of the church, in front of a couple dozen high school students and parents, that I realized something that has literally changed my life.

Before I left for Haiti, I had prayed and prayed that I would be prepared to witness whatever great things God might have in store for me and my team. The driving force behind these prayers was the anticipation that God was going to show up in a huge, mind-blowing kind of way. Simply because He could.

Reflecting back on my prayer that night at youth group about a week after returning to the States, it finally dawned on me.

Sure, I saw God do amazing things in Haiti. My team and I had been granted so many opportunities to witness that "above and beyond all you can ask or imagine" kind of stuff promised in Ephesians 3. However, God does not limit Himself to working in the far off country of Haiti. The God who carried buses and protected his children there is the very same God who longs to walk with me (and you) each and every day of our lives here – through the soccer games, the cancer diagnoses, the daily provisions we often take for granted. All we have to do is open our eyes so that we might see the miracles He is performing and the lives He is transforming daily.

And since returning from Haiti, that has been my goal – to see Him at work all around me – both in the ordinary days and the extraordinary ones.

Some of the moments in this book are really recent, while others are years old. It has, quite simply, taken this long for me to realize the blessing that each one of them truly has been in this thing called life. To this day, these moments leave me speechless, in teary awe and wonder, of the graciousness of my God.

> *My prayer is that after witnessing the hand of our ever-present, awe-inspiring God reflected across the pages of this book, you will pause to be still before Him and that you, too, would begin watching for and expecting to encounter His presence in all of the places you find yourself in this crazy adventure called life.*

So there it is. This book isn't about me or my stories. It's about a really big God and His story. God has always been working on my behalf, as He has on yours, but it took me being almost 1,200 miles from home in a village tucked into the side of Haitian mountains to recognize God's relentless pursuit of me through His daily moments of grace. He showed me that He's in the big things, the far away things, but also in the small things, the next door or down the street things.

The book you hold in your hands is a collection of moments, based on true stories, that have occurred either in my life or the lives of my family or friends. Each defining moment, the miracle upon which the story hinges, has in no way been altered; however, all names and some places, none of which compromise the truth of the message, have been changed to respect the privacy and anonymity of the individuals involved.

So now, we embark. I encourage you to work your way through these pages with the understanding that God doesn't limit the gift of

His miracles to my life or the lives of those I know. He lavishes grace, these moments, on the lives of *all* His children. He's doing it for you, even now. As it was five years ago, my prayer remains that this book points you to our God and the moments He moves in little ways as reminders of His love – just because He can.

Before I Even Knew You

James 5:15-16 – And the prayer offered in faith will make the sick person well; the Lord will raise him up. Therefore confess your sins to each other and pray for each other so that you may be healed. The prayer of a righteous man is powerful and effective.

    Katie stood beside the stove, stirring a pot of macaroni and cheese. She saw the reflection of her face staring back at her from the side of the metal pot and sighed. Her eyes looked tired. Even the freckles that dotted her cheeks and the bridge of her nose appeared fainter than normal.

Katie watched the orange slices of cheese melt and mix with the milk, but her mind wasn't focused on her cooking tonight. It was still on the phone, talking with the receptionist at the doctor's office who had called earlier in the day.

"Hey, give that back! It's mine."

"But I was using it. You're supposed to share, remember?"

Katie heard her sons bickering in the other room but couldn't summon the energy to referee another fight. It was a constant battle between the five- and eleven-year-old.

Another voice, higher-pitched and commanding, interrupted the squabble. "Guys, please stop fighting. Just take turns, okay?"

Katie smiled. At thirteen, her daughter was the oldest of the three children. She was a peacekeeper by nature and a lifesaver when it came to intervening in the boys' constant arguments.

Katie set the plastic spoon she was cooking with on the edge of the sink. Placing her elbows on the countertops, she closed her eyes and let her head rest in her hands.

Moments later, Katie heard the back door slide open. Her husband's feet pounded against the doormat as he shook the loose dirt from his shoes.

I meant to move the kids' shoes from out of the doorway. John hates when they're scattered right in front of the door, Katie thought.

"With all the shoes at the door, you'd think a small army lived here, not just us and the kids," John called from the other room.

Katie heard John set his briefcase on the kitchen table, but she didn't raise her head.

"Honey, are you okay?" John asked as he rushed across the small kitchen and bent down next to Katie. "I was just kidding about the shoes."

She turned to look at him, her eyes welling with tears. She couldn't answer.

"Let me say 'hi' to the kids and put my briefcase in my office, then let's talk, okay?" John asked as he enveloped Katie in his arms.

She nodded, wiping the corners of her eyes with the back of her hand. Turning back to the stove, Katie slipped the green been casserole into the oven and turned off the stove burner heating the macaroni. She heard John talking to their daughter, Charlotte, in the other room.

"Charlotte, could you do a favor for me?" John asked.

"Yes, Daddy, of course."

"Would you make sure the guys are okay for a few minutes? Mommy and I are going to step outside and check on the chicken that's on the grill."

"Yes, sir. Everything in here will be A-Okay," Charlotte said. Katie imagined the girl wrapping her arms around John's neck and kissing his scruffy cheek.

John reentered the kitchen and wordlessly took Katie's hand, leading her to the back deck.

"Honey, what's wrong?" John asked as he turned her toward him and let his hands rest on each side of her small waist. He brushed a strand of her shoulder length brown hair behind her ear.

A few tears escaped Katie's eyes and trickled down her face. She wiped them away with the back of her hand and let a sigh slip from between her lips.

"Jeanine called today," she said.

John's brow furrowed in confusion as he ran a hand through his dark brown hair. Katie realized he was trying to figure out whom Jeanine was and if he should know her. His puzzled expression forced a quiet laugh to slip through her lips.

"I'm sorry. Let me try that again. Jeanine, the secretary from the doctor's office, called today," she said and drew a shaky breath.

Realization flooded John's eyes, and he pulled Katie close to his chest. He rested his chin on the top of her head and spoke into her hair. "It wasn't good news." The words were more a statement than a question.

A sob caught in Katie's throat, and she shook her head while she waited for the words to come. John tightened his grip on her thin frame and waited patiently, stroking her back with his thumb.

"It's okay, sweetheart. Can you tell me exactly what the nurse said?"

After a few moments, the sobs subsided, and Katie lifted her eyes to her husband. "She said that the doctor wants to see me again as soon as possible. She wouldn't tell me anything other than that some of the numbers from my tests came back higher than normal and that the doctor expects to see me back in his office by the end of the week."

"Okay, then we'll make an appointment. I'll call first thing in the morning if you'd like me to," John said.

Katie bit her lip and looked into the face of her husband, thankful that his expression held nothing but love and determination. "Actually, that won't be necessary," she said.

"Honey, if the doctor wants to see you again, you have to go," John said, his voice strained.

"Oh, I know that, and I will. I just meant you don't need to call for an appointment." Katie paused before continuing. "Because I already did."

A small smile flashed across John's face. "Of course you did. When is it?"

"Tomorrow afternoon." Katie watched John's eyebrows rise and his mouth drop open a little. "But I can go alone. I know that's really short notice and you probably have a lot going on at work."

"I know that you *can* go alone, but you absolutely *will* not. No meetings or appointments at work are so important that they cannot be rearranged," John said resolutely. He shifted his glasses on his nose and pulled Katie into a hug. She was short, which allowed him to rest his chin on her head. "Nothing will keep me from being beside you. Not now and not ever."

*

The next afternoon, Katie wiggled around in the waiting room chair, trying to find a comfortable position. The room was small, with pictures of generic blue, yellow, and pink flower bouquets hung at random on the walls. Only one other couple sat in the room, huddled in the opposite corner.

Katie closed her eyes and leaned her head back against the wall. A moment later, she felt a warm hand on her leg. She peeked through one eye as John plopped down in the chair next to her.

"How's my girl holding up?" he whispered.

Katie offered him a weak smile. "She's scared. She never really thought she'd have to do this again."

"Then how about we pray," John suggested. "Because I'm pretty scared, too."

Katie let John take her hands in his and bowed her head. John prayed aloud, asking the Lord for good test results, but most of all for His will to be done.

"We know that whatever the outcome, You are in this. You promised to lead and guide us and never forsake us. We're trusting you, Jesus. Thank you for your promises. Amen."

John moved his hand and intertwined his fingers with Katie's. When he leaned his head back against the wall, she closed her eyes.

How did we end up here, Lord? She wondered silently.

When she opened them again, John was staring right at her. A soft smile tugged at the corners of his lips, lessening the dark circles that had formed under his eyes almost overnight. Katie hated causing him to worry.

"What are you thinking about?" she asked.

"Just you. Only you. Always you," John said and planted a quick kiss on her cheek.

A nurse dressed in dark blue scrubs opened the door and called into the crowded waiting room. "Mrs. Aldridge?"

Katie stood up and slipped her purse over her shoulder. Her eyes met John's as he stood and reached for her hand. Together they walked toward the nurse standing in the doorway.

The nurse's name was Marcia. She led them down a series of hallways that seemed to turn back on themselves. They passed several nurses' stations, all sterilized and without the smallest speck of dirt or dust on them. Finally, the nurse stopped in front of a closed wooden door at the end of one of the hallways. She knocked twice then pushed the door open far enough to peer inside. Content that the room was indeed empty, the nurse opened the door wide enough for John and Katie to enter.

"Dr. Caller will be with you shortly," she said as she put Katie's file in the holder on the back of the door and closed it as she left.

Katie set her purse on the floor by a chair that looked as if it had been wedged into the corner of the room before climbing onto the examining table beside it. John leaned back against the table, examining one of the many informational posters hanging on the walls that described this or that illness.

Besides the posters, the room was sparsely decorated and contained only a sink, some cabinets, and a rolling chair. The room was eerily quiet, as if it, too, was holding its breath. Katie dangled her legs over the edge of the table and let them swing back and forth to the ticking of her watch.

John nudged Katie's knee with his hip and turned to look at her. He opened his mouth to speak, but before the words could come out, they heard a knock on the door as it was simultaneously pushed open.

"Dr. Caller," the raspy voice of an elderly gentleman said.

Dr. Caller was in his mid-sixties. He wore a white coat, which almost exactly matched the white tufts of hair that grew up from around his ears. A stethoscope hung from around his neck, and in his hands he held the clipboard with Katie's records.

"Katie. John." He nodded to each of them in turn.

"Dr. Caller," John said in reply.

Time seemed to stand still as Dr. Caller reached for the chair at the sink and rolled it around to face the couple. He sat down in the chair and leaned back as he glanced at the chart in his hands. Katie sneaked a glance at her husband who was also watching the doctor intently, waiting to hear what he had to say.

"There is no easy way to tell you this, and you know I'm not one to sugar-coat the truth," Dr. Caller began. "So I won't."

John reached for Katie's hand and held it firmly.

"We received the results from the biopsy yesterday afternoon. The lab was able to run the same test twice with the sample we collected last week, but the results were the same both times. I'm sorry. Your cancer has returned."

*

Cheryl rinsed the soap off her hands and dried them on a paper towel. She turned to her children who were playing on the floor behind her.

"Okay, kids, run along outside and play for a little while. Mommy and Daddy are going to talk with the other adults for a few minutes," Cheryl said as she bent down to tie her daughter's shoe. Obediently, the girl guided her two brothers toward the back door, her long brown hair trailing halfway down her back.

Cheryl stood at the window and watched her three children join in a game of tag with the other kids already running around the fenced in backyard. She balanced her youngest daughter on her hip, the child's head resting Cheryl's shoulder.

A woman joined Cheryl at the window. "Cheryl? We're about to start the discussion. Are you and your husband going to join us?" she asked.

Cheryl smiled and tucked her short blond hair behind her ears with her free hand. "Yes, of course. Remind me of your name again?"

"I'm Michelle," the woman said as she placed a hand on Cheryl's shoulder.

Cheryl cast one last glance at the chaos in the backyard before turning to follow Michelle into the living room where the couples' home group Bible study was meeting. "Michelle, are you sure the kids will be okay alone out there?"

Michelle nodded, causing her black ponytail to bounce. "They're completely safe. The entire yard is fenced in, and there's a child safety lock on the gate," she said. "Plus, we hired my fifteen-year-old daughter and her best friend to watch them. The condition of their payment? That no one gets hurt or runs into the house crying."

Cheryl laughed. "Works for me."

She followed Michelle into the living room and sat beside her husband on the blue futon that matched the lacy curtains hanging from the windows. Cheryl studied the room, noting that all the decorations, from the furniture to the paintings hanging on the walls, were some shade of blue.

"I think everybody's here." Michelle's words interrupted Cheryl's thoughts. "So let's go ahead and get started. I hope you all had a chance to meet Blake and Cheryl over hors d'oeuvres. They're new to the church and are testing out different home groups to find the one that is best for their family."

Cheryl leaned against her husband and smiled at the other couples around the circle.

"While you're all taking out your Bibles and discussion questions, let's go ahead and share prayer requests with the group." Michelle paused, then continued. "And actually, I have an urgent one to share with you."

Around the circle, the rustling of papers stilled as all attention was directed at Michelle and the request she needed to share.

"The request is for a young mother I met through our homeschooling co-op. She's one of the sweetest ladies I know. She's in her mid-thirties, and she and her husband have three children ages thirteen, eleven, and five."

Those are just about the same ages as my children, Cheryl thought as she jotted notes onto the backside of an index card she found stuck in the middle of her Bible.

"The mom's name is Katie. Some of you may remember the prayer request I shared with you several years ago when she was first diagnosed with breast cancer," Michelle continued.

Cheryl looked up from her notecard long enough to notice several heads nodding.

Michelle took a deep breath. "I talked with her husband, John, earlier today. They met with her oncologist this afternoon. He confirmed that her cancer has returned."

Cheryl's eyes filled with tears. *God, I don't even know this woman, but my heart is so broken for her and her family*, Cheryl prayed.

Cheryl tried to focus on the remaining prayer requests shared and the discussion that took place over the next half hour, but her mind kept returning to Katie and her family. She couldn't imagine being in the young woman's place, but she decided that from that moment on, she would pray for Katie as fervently as if she knew her.

*

Four months later, Cheryl woke up in a cold sweat. She glanced over at her husband, who was fast asleep and snoring. *Thank you, Lord. The last thing he needs is me waking him up at all hours of the night*, Cheryl prayed as she rolled quietly out of bed and fitted her feet into a pair of slippers.

She tiptoed out of the bedroom, pulling the door closed gently behind her. After checking on the kids and pulling her youngest daughter's blankets back up over her little body, Cheryl curled up on the cushioned window seat in her upstairs office.

Leaning her head against the cool glass pane, Cheryl closed her eyes and prayed, just as she had each night for the past four months.

Father, I don't know why, but my heart is so burdened for Katie and her family. I can't begin to imagine what she's going through or the fear and uncertainty that must be plaguing those precious children. But I do know that You hold them in Your hands, and nothing that happens to them has not passed before You first.

An hour later, Cheryl climbed back into bed and slipped her feet under the covers. As she drifted off to sleep, Cheryl continued praying for Katie's peace of mind and strength to face the days ahead. But more than anything, she prayed for a miracle.

*

Katie adjusted her wig and looked in the mirror one final time. Out of the corner of her eye, she noticed John watching her from the bedroom where he was pulling on his socks and sticking his feet into his shoes.

A weary smile creased her face as she leaned through the doorway and met his gaze. "And just what are you staring at so intently?" she called across the room to her husband.

He stood and made his way toward her, giving her a quick peck on the forehead. "Only the strongest, most beautiful woman I've ever laid eyes on," he quipped.

Katie couldn't suppress a smile. John grew serious and held her out at arms' length. He bent down just slightly so that he stood at eye level with his wife. "Seriously, honey. Not only have you amazed the doctors over the past year, but you've also amazed me. I could not be more proud of you, of your strength and your spirit." He wrapped his arms around her and held her tight.

Katie laid her head on his shoulder and whispered, "Thank you. It wasn't me. It was God. And it was you. And it was the constant prayers of our friends."

Katie's thoughts drifted back to the special prayer service that had been arranged for her in the weeks following her original diagnosis. Some of the women in her Sunday school class at church had immediately started an around-the-clock prayer vigil and had invited many of Katie's closest friends and family members to a private service in the old chapel at her church. Those closest to Katie had spent hours surrounding her in prayer and anointing her with oil, asking God for a miracle.

Katie breathed out a long, slow sigh. *That day seems so long ago, and in some respects I guess it was. Time has a funny way of flying by and slowing down, and a year can seem both like yesterday and a million days away.*

The phone rang in the background, shaking Katie from her thoughts. She looked up at her husband. "That's probably my mom wondering if we're still coming. Are the kids ready to go?"

He cocked his head and shrugged a shoulder. "If you're asking if they have had breakfast and if they're all still alive, then yes," he replied with the same dorky grin he'd been sporting since his high school days.

Katie feigned shock and answered the phone. "Hello?"

When she heard her mother's voice on the other end of the line she nodded. John left the room to pair up three kids with their coats and shoes. Katie smiled, watching him go. The path their marriage had taken was far from anything she had imagined as a twenty-year-old starting out, but she knew she wouldn't have traded a moment of it for the world.

*

"Okay, guys, we'll see you in a little while," Katie called over her shoulder to the three children standing beside her mother.

Charlotte had just recently celebrated a twelfth birthday and ever being mommy's little helper, she held her youngest brother on her hip. Their middle child stood beside Charlotte holding his grandmother's hand, all four of them waving to the couple as Katie joined John in the front seat of the van.

An hour later, they were back in the waiting room they had frequented all too often over the past year, and while they could have let their fear overwhelm them, Katie and John chose to trust the God who was bigger.

Katie looked around the almost empty waiting room. Only four other people were waiting this morning, a middle-aged couple in their fifties and two women, one old and gray and the other not more than twenty-five, with short auburn locks that framed her face. Katie wondered about their stories.

John nudged her gently with his elbow. "What're you looking at, honey?" he asked as he followed her gaze with his eyes.

"The two women," she whispered, not wanting the pair to overhear her. "I can't help but wonder about their story. About which one of them is here as the patient and which is the care-giver." Katie looked at her husband, her eyes burning.

He took her hand and lifted it to his lips. "Always my tender-hearted girl," he said with a smile.

"Mrs. Aldridge?" a voice called from the doorway.

Katie looked up and did a double take when she saw the familiar face from the year before. It appeared that the nurse hadn't changed much in a year, though her long brown hair had more streaks of gray than before. The nurse's breath caught in her throat when she recognized Katie, but a warm smile filled her face in the next moment.

Katie and John met her at the door.

"You look so good!" the nurse exclaimed as she gave Katie a quick hug.

"Thank you, Marcia," Katie said.

"If you two will follow me," Marcia said as she led them to an empty room. "The doctor will be right with y-"

"The doctor is right here," Dr. Caller said as he stepped into the room and took the clipboard from Marcia. There was a twinkle in his eye that hadn't been there a year ago.

Katie looked at John and couldn't stop the smile that was spreading across her face or the hope that was taking root in her heart.

Marcia quickly left the room, and Dr. Caller leaned back against the door. He flipped the front page of Katie's chart over the clipboard and set his glasses squarely on his nose. His eyes darted back and forth across the pages as he studied the notes written on the paper. He started speaking before his eyes left the pages in front of him.

"Katie, after your Stage II recurrence last year, I didn't think this day would come. With your family history covered in cancer and its appearance in your body, not once, but twice, at such a young age, the chances for recovery were slim," Dr. Caller said. He looked up and his gaze passed from Katie to her husband.

"But," he continued, "I am happy to tell you that the test results from last week indicate that the chemotherapy and radiation treatments have removed the cancer from your body."

Tears of joy spilled down Katie's cheeks. When she turned to look at her husband, she couldn't help but laugh because his face was wet as well. She embraced him while Dr. Caller allowed them the moment to celebrate.

Then he spoke again. "I know you realize how important it is to celebrate this milestone. We've done so before. But I would be failing you as your doctor if I didn't give a word of caution as you move forward."

Katie wiped her eyes with the back of her hand and placed it on John's shoulder as they turned their attention fully to Dr. Caller.

"While we see no traces of the cancer in your body now, the chance of a recurrence in the months and years to come is higher since you've battled the disease twice already. As before, until you reach the five-year mark of being cancer-free, we will term your case as 'in remission,' meaning that the cancer has either been eliminated or suppressed. If you make it five years without the cancer returning, we'll officially declare you free of cancer," Dr. Caller said.

Katie nodded but said nothing.

"In the meantime, you'll come see me every three months for the next year and every six months after that," Dr. Caller finished.

Katie closed her eyes and let the reality sink in. She was cancer-free again, at least for the time being. She didn't know what the future would hold, but the choice was hers: she could worry about it or enjoy it. Her eyes met John's as they stood to leave the examining room, and she was overcome by the love she saw in them. She took his hand and decided then and there that she was going to celebrate every moment of this second chance she had been given.

*

Two years after the night Cheryl and her husband had visited the first home group, she found herself sitting in a circle much like that one, though this circle was comprised only of women. Instead of an evening spent with other couples, Cheryl had recently found her place in a Wednesday morning Bible study group. Each week, Cheryl and the eleven ladies in her group laughed and cried together, sharing prayer requests and praise reports.

As Cheryl leafed through her Bible, searching for the passage the group was preparing to discuss, an index card slipped out from the pages of her Bible and fluttered to the floor. She leaned over and grabbed the card. Before she stuck it back in her Bible, she glanced at the notes scrawled across the back of the card and saw Katie's name. *I wonder where she is today, Lord. Did you heal her?*

A woman two seats to Cheryl's left addressed their leader. "Ashley, I know we usually share prayer requests and praises after the discussion, but there's something I feel like I should share before we begin," the woman said. She pushed a strand of her short brown hair behind her ear, but it fell right back into her eye.

Ashley smiled. "Go right ahead."

"All of you know that I've been battling a recurrence of breast cancer for the past year," the woman paused, her eyes filling with tears. "Well, I received word from my doctor yesterday that all traces of the cancerous cells have been removed from my body."

Whispered prayers of gratitude, claps, and cheers erupted from the circle of women. Those sitting close enough patted the woman on the back, while others smiled and lifted their hands in praise.

Cheryl thought about the story this woman had shared with the group over the past several weeks. The woman had mentioned that she had three children: a high schooler, a middle schooler, and a first grader. She had mentioned that her fortieth birthday was approaching and that she was anticipating the milestone and the life it symbolized rather than dreading it like so many others did. The woman had told the group that she was battling cancer and that her hair was actually a wig. *God, it can't possibly be her, can it?*

Cheryl couldn't contain her curiosity any longer. She had to know. "You had cancer," she blurted out.

The woman looked at her, stunned. "I did."

"You are the person I have been praying for," Cheryl said, her voice cracking.

The woman's eyes filled with tears. "I am?"

Cheryl stood and placed her Bible and notebook on the chair behind her. She walked over to the woman, who rose to meet her. Taking the woman's shoulders in her hands, Cheryl looked into the woman's eyes. "You are Katie. You are the person God has been writing on my heart for the past year. Only He could do something like this." She pulled Katie close and whispered in her ear. "I prayed for you before I even knew you, and I will continue to pray for you now that I do."

Just Like in the Movies

Matthew 19:26 – Jesus looked at them and said, "With man this is impossible, but with God all things are possible."

    Coach Middleton blew her whistle, signaling the beginning of practice. Kaley shot one last three-pointer, but instead of slipping through the net, it circled the rim twice before bouncing out. Her shoulders dropped in frustration.
    "Unlucky," Coach Middleton called from where she stood watching at the other end of the court.

Kaley glanced over her shoulder at her high school coach before chasing down the basketball. She wedged it between her legs so she could retie her long, straight blond hair into a ponytail. She felt the top of her hair for bumps and, satisfied that it was smooth, tied her hot pink ribbon around the rubber band.

Twelve ponytails bounced as the girls gathered all the basketballs scattered around the gymnasium during warm up and jogged over to where Coach Middleton stood waiting for them, clipboard under her arm.

At first glance, Coach Middleton didn't really look like a basketball coach, and technically she wasn't. Her specialty was soccer, but the previous basketball coach had accepted a position at a larger school in Georgia so the small private school Kaley attended had given the role to whoever would volunteer for the job.

Coach Middleton was barely five feet tall. Her brown hair was cut short around her ears, and she wore glasses instead of contacts. Kaley had met Coach Middleton for the first time over the summer. The woman was her third basketball coach in as many seasons.

"All right, ladies. Take a couple of laps around the gym to warm up. Then Kaley will lead you in stretches," Coach Middleton said.

She turned to Kaley. "Let's not spend more than ten or fifteen minutes on warm up, okay? You guys have already been shooting around, and we've got a lot to cover today."

"Yes, ma'am, got it," Kaley said.

The only senior, Kaley was the captain of the varsity team at Pineview Christian School. An athlete by nature, she played every sport from softball to competing on the track team. By far, however, basketball was her favorite. Kaley only stood five and a half feet tall, but she could play any position on the court. While her preferred position was shooting guard, she'd been known to post up on the block as a forward or bring the ball up the court as the point guard.

She turned to address the team. "All right, ladies, let's start with a nice easy jog around the gym."

The gymnasium at Bethlehem Methodist Church was nothing special. While it didn't even have room to roll bleachers onto the sidelines, the building was equipped with all the essentials: lines painted on the floor, two basketball goals, air conditioning, and a water fountain. It was also at the disposal of the team free of charge. The church graciously lent the private school team the building for two hours each Monday, Tuesday, and Thursday afternoon for practice.

The women's basketball program at Pineview Christian School had never had a history of being a top competitor in the region. However, it had made the first round of playoffs in the not-so-distant past. That was during Jennifer's era. Jennifer was possibly the most skilled player on the women's side of the basketball since the school's inception. Things had drastically changed in the athletics department in the years since she graduated. Most days, a ten-point loss was considered a victory.

"Kaley, could you stay for a few minutes after practice today?" Coach Middleton asked during a water break between drills. "There's something I'd like to talk to you about."

"Sure, Coach. No problem," she replied between gulps of water. "Is this about state?"

For years, Kaley had dreamed of playing in the state tournament, but so far, she'd never had the chance. At the beginning of the year, Kaley had told Coach Middleton about her aspirations for the team, and the two had talked about the post-season tournament at the end of almost every practice.

"Great, and actually, it's not. Meet me outside by my car once you've changed." Coach Middleton looked at her clipboard before blowing her whistle. "All right, ladies. Let's run through our offense one more time. Then we'll spend the rest of practice scrimmaging full court."

Her eyes turned to Kaley, but she continued addressing the whole team. "Kaley's group needs to set up on defense. I want you to practice in the position you will play in during a game. If you're a forward, don't try to play a point guard right now. Understand?"

Twelve heads bobbed.

"All right, the rest of you come with me. We'll set up the offense and see if we can't run through it a couple times to get all the kinks out," Coach Middleton said.

The rest of practice flew by, but Kaley couldn't stop thinking about Coach Middleton's request. It wasn't unusual that Coach had asked her to hang around and talk for a few minutes after practice. They did that almost every day anyway, tossing around ideas for plays or discussing what skills the team still needed to work on. What puzzled Kaley was that she had asked to speak to her outside, away from everyone else.

What could she need to talk to me about that is so secretive? Kaley wondered as practice drew to an end.

"All right, ladies. Great work today," Coach Middleton said. "Who knows when our next game is?"

"Isn't it Monday at Shiloh?" Sophie, the lone junior on the team, asked. At five-foot-nine she was far from a giant, but she was the tallest girl on the team by at least three inches.

"That's right. Thanks, Sophie," Coach Middleton said. "No practice tomorrow, but we'll be back at it Thursday. Maybe shoot around on your own tomorrow afternoon to stay loose."

Sophie raised her hand, flipping her long, brown ponytail back over her shoulder. "Coach, are we practicing Friday afternoon, too?"

"How about we wait and make that call after Thursday's practice. I'll let you know," Coach Middleton said. "All right, Kaley. They're all yours."

Kaley looked around at the faces around her, still red from exertion. "Okay, ladies, let's bring it in. Lady Flames on three. One. Two. Three..."

"Lady Flames!" the team said in unison.

As the girls started gathering their things and putting the basketballs back in the mesh ball bag, Kaley threw on a hoodie and some sweatpants and ran outside to find Coach

Middleton putting equipment in the trunk of her silver Toyota Avalon.

"Hey, Coach. You wanted to talk?" she asked.

"Yes, Kaley. I have an idea," Coach Middleton said, the corners of her eyes crinkling as she smiled. "How about we have a team watch party Friday night instead of practice?"

"A team watch party?" Kaley asked. "You *want* to revisit our last game? Against Anderson?"

Kaley thought back to the thirty-point beating her team had suffered at the hands of the Lady Lions. She knew watching game film could be valuable, but there were some games that were better left in the past. That had been one of those games.

"No no no." Coach Middleton laughed. "Not a watch party for game film. I was thinking more along the lines of inspirational film, maybe try to encourage the team. Say, *Facing the Giants*?"

"Wow! Really? That's my favorite movie!" Kaley exclaimed.

Coach Middleton laughed. "I know it is. You tell me just about every day how much that movie inspires you."

Kaley smiled and shrugged. "You're right. I just love the message – that when we cry out to the Lord for help in the middle of our uncertainty or hopelessness, He hears and answers. I know the girls will love it! In fact, we could have everybody over to my house and even order pizza," Kaley said, excited at the turn of events.

"Why don't you check with your mom first," Coach Middleton suggested. "But I think that sounds like a great idea."

"Me, too," Kaley said as a huge spread across her face. "They're going to love the movie AND a day off of practice. When are you going to tell them?"

"I'll send out an email to all of the parents tonight, letting them know that we won't have practice on Friday after school but that their daughters do need to reserve a few hours that night for basketball. How about we wait and announce to the team exactly what we'll be doing that evening at the end of practice Thursday?" Coach Middleton asked.

"That sounds perfect! Secrets are hard to keep, but this one will be so worth it! Thanks, Coach," Kaley said.

*

Kaley was helping her teammates arrange their sleeping bags and blankets on the carpeted den floor when she heard a knock come from the other room. She jumped up from where she knelt in the corner and stepped over several of her teammates, who were dressed in t-shirts and patterned pajama pants, as she crossed the room to see who was at the door. On her way through the kitchen, Kaley passed Coach Middleton carrying two bowls of popcorn.

"You about ready to start the movie?" Coach asked.

Kaley nodded. "Sure am. The girls are getting situated in their sleeping bags and under blankets. I think they're ready to do some work on that popcorn."

Coach Middleton laughed. "I have no doubt. I've seen you girls eat. Where are you going?"

"I heard a knock. Sophie's the only one not here yet, so I'm hoping it's her," Kaley said.

She jogged across the sunroom tile floor and unlocked the sliding glass door. Sophie smiled and waved, a two-liter soda tucked under her arm.

"Hi, Kaley. Sorry I'm late," Sophie said as she stepped inside the house and slipped off her shoes.

"You're right on time. We're just about to start the movie," Kaley said, squeezing her teammate's shoulders and leading the way to the den.

Two hours later, as the movie's credits scrolled, Kaley glanced at the faces of her teammates. Several girls wiped tears from their eyes, and the sound of sniffles rose from all corners of the room. Kaley dabbed the corners of her eyes with the sleeve of her shirt before meeting Coach Middleton's gaze from where she sat on the end of the tan leather couch. When her coach nodded, Kaley turned the television off and flipped the nearest light switch.

"Well, ladies, what did you think of the movie?" Coach Middleton asked.

The room was quiet for several minutes. Finally, Emily, a freshman with long brown hair, freckles, and bright blue eyes spoke. Her soft words filled the silence of the room. "I liked it," she paused. "In a lot of ways I think it's kind of like our team."

"I think it's a lot like our team," Coach Middleton agreed. "Anyone else?"

Around the room, heads nodded.

Sophie turned to Kaley. "This is the movie you were telling me about a while back, isn't it?"

Kaley smiled. "Yeah, it is. I got to see a special premiere of the movie, before it was even out in theaters, and I haven't been able to get the message behind the movie out of my head."

"I think it'll be a long time before I forget it, too," Emily said. "I can't really relate to the couple's infertility, but I definitely understand Coach Taylor's search for meaning and purpose in the midst of the storms threatening to overtake him."

"And God answered, overwhelming Coach Taylor with little reminders that nothing is impossible with Him," Sophie chimed in. She turned to Coach Middleton. "Hey, Coach? Do you think we could make that our motto, too? You know, that nothing is impossible with God? We don't need to win football games, but we could sure use some help on the basketball court if we're going to get Kaley to state."

Kaley couldn't stop the tears filling her eyes from spilling down her cheeks. She was already nodding when Coach Middleton looked at her with eyebrows raised. "Kaley, you're the captain. What do you think?"

Kaley smiled through the tears, her eyes meeting the gaze of each of her teammates. Swallowing past the lump in her throat, Kaley whispered. "I'd love nothing more than for that to be our team's mantra for the rest of the season."

*

Kaley had hoped that the movie would be the extra push her team needed to break out of the mediocre and begin playing inspired basketball that would win games. After another week of loss after loss, Kaley cornered Coach Middleton at the end of practice one afternoon.

"Hey, Coach. Could I talk to you for a minute?" she asked.

Coach Middleton looked up from her cell phone and nodded before tucking the device into the pocket of her sweatpants. "Sure thing. What's up?"

"I know that I want to win games, and I think that the rest of the team does, too," Kaley said.

"I would agree with both of those statements," Coach Middleton said.

"Okay, good. So I think that the reality of the situation is that as much as we want to win, we lack the skill set to be a powerhouse team. I was wondering if maybe we could change up our strategy a little bit?"

Coach Middleton crossed her arms and tilted her head to one side. "What do you have in mind?"

"Instead of trying to learn these fancy plays, which are good, just really complicated, I think it would be more beneficial to spend time reviewing the basics and trying to perfect the fundamentals of the game. Maybe if we worked on form shooting, running the basic offensive plays we already know, and making sure we're in the best physical shape possible, we'll have a better payoff on the court?" Kaley offered.

Coach Middleton nodded. "You know, I've been considering that very thing. I know you're still hoping for a berth in the state tournament. I am, too. But I think it's time we come to grips with the fact that if we're going to win, it's not going to be because we're naturally gifted or even the better team."

"Exactly. Any games we win are going to be the direct result of the hard work we put in before the first whistle blows and our refusal to give up. Well, and maybe a little help from God," Kaley finished.

*

Finally, about two-thirds of the way through her senior season and two weeks after Kaley's talk with Coach Middleton, everything clicked for the Pineview team.

They were playing away at Millcreek Academy, about an hour and a half drive away from Pineview. Millcreek was ranked first in the conference, and their star player had already signed on to play at the collegiate level as a freshman the following year.

At the end of the game, Kaley looked up at the scoreboard and hung her head in defeat. *I just watched every one of my teammates play the game of her life, God. But we still came up three points short of the win. I don't know what else we can do.*

Kaley sat on the top row of bleachers during the varsity boys' basketball game, replaying each minute of the girls' game in her head. Coach Middleton climbed up the wooden bleachers and sat beside her. She placed a hand on Kaley's knee. "You okay, kiddo?"

Kaley took a deep breath. "I think I will be. I'm just disappointed, I guess. I really thought we had them tonight."

Coach Middleton nodded. "I thought we did, too. If I had asked any one of you at halftime who was going to win the game, I know, without a doubt, that each of you would have said we were."

"Yeah, that's the thing. I know they all wanted it. I just can't figure out how this fits in with everything we've been talking about – the movie and our motto, you know? I thought nothing was supposed to be impossible with God. So why did we still lose? Shouldn't God have given us the win?" Kaley asked, her eyes searching her coach's face for answers.

"Kaley, I know you're disappointed with how the game ended tonight. But I think God is trying to teach you something here," Coach Middleton said gently.

"You do?"

"I do. In the movie, God didn't work miracles for Coach Taylor because He had to. He worked them because Coach Taylor had faith and believed. God rewarded him for his faith. God answered his prayers, not because He had to, but because He wanted to. Coach Taylor was faithful in asking and continued to believe in God's goodness regardless of the circumstances," Coach Middleton said. "Tell me this. How did Coach Taylor's team make the playoffs?"

Kaley thought for a moment. "They got a call the day after the region game they lost, saying that the other team had cheated and was disqualified."

"Exactly," Coach Middleton said as she wrapped an arm around Kaley's shoulders. "That kind of thing doesn't happen every day. But Coach Taylor was faithful, and God rewarded that in extraordinary ways."

Kaley wiped at a tear that was snaking down her cheek. "So you're saying I still have to believe?" she asked.

Coach Middleton laid her arm across Kaley's shoulders. "That's exactly what I'm saying. With the loss tonight, we have to win the first game of the region tournament to earn a bid to the state tourney. You and I both know that's a long shot. But tell me, Kaley, what is impossible with God?"

Kaley smiled. "Nothing, Coach. Nothing is impossible."

*

A week later, Kaley and her teammates were back in the Millcreek gym, ready for a rematch. This game held more weight than the first one, however, as the winner would be guaranteed a seed in the state tournament. With the less than average season Pineview had endured and a losing record overall, a victory was the only way they would make the post-season tournament. Period.

"Ladies, bring it in," Coach Middleton called from the bench. The buzzer sounded, officially ending the pre-game warm up period. Kaley and her teammates circled around their coach. She glanced over at Millcreek's bench and saw them doing the same.

Kaley turned her attention back to her team's huddle as Coach Middleton said, "I want you to remember how far we've come this season, how far God has brought us. Play your best, but leave everything on the court."

Kaley's eyes connected with her coach's.

"And Kaley, play like it's your last. Make every second count."

She nodded, too caught up in what could be the final pre-game huddle of her basketball career to say anything.

"Now tell me, Lady Flames, what is impossible with God?" Coach Middleton asked.

The girls looked at one another and smiled before answering in unison, "Nothing!"

The buzzer sounded three quick times, summoning the teams to the sideline so that the starters could be announced. Before she knew it, Kaley was high-fiving the other team's players as they prepared for the jump ball, and just like that, the game was underway.

The game was everything Kaley had dreamed it would be. Her teammates hit shots they'd never made before and hustled for steals with renewed energy and vigor. Kaley didn't know if it was just a lucky night or if their passion was the result of the unspoken urgency of continuing her high school career. Her teammates knew that she'd never played in the state tournament and how badly she wanted the team to make it that year. They knew that this game could be the last time she'd ever play with them.

The crowd counted down the final seconds. Five. Four. Three. Two. One. The buzzer sounded one last time. Cheers erupted from the stands as fans rushed the court. Millcreek's fans.

Kaley looked up at the scoreboard. 41-39. Two points separated the winner and loser. Kaley had missed the state tournament by one basket.

*

Four days later, Kaley sat in the back of Bible class, surrounded by her classmates. She stifled a yawn. The fifth period class was always the hardest to stay awake during because it was right after lunch. Kaley held a pink highlighter over her textbook and listened to her teacher's instructions.

"Okay, class. Now skip down seven lines and highlight the paragraph that starts with..."

"Excuse me, Mr. Tipton?" The question drifted into the classroom from the hallway.

Kaley looked up to see the school's secretary, Miss Fischer, standing in the doorway of Mr. Tipton's classroom. Miss Fischer was probably in her early thirties, with short brown hair that hung limply by her face. As usual, she was holding the black walkie-talkie she carried with her everywhere. It was probably a good habit, though. Everyone knew that Miss Fischer was the one who kept the school running, even if she was technically only employed as the secretary.

"Oh, hello, Miss Fischer," Mr. Tipton said. "Can I do something for you?"

Mr. Tipton was the Bible teacher at Pineview Christian School. He was lovingly called Bibleman after the evangelical superhero, and his deep laugh was loved by his students. The top of his head was balding, but the dark brown hair he still had clung to the sides of his head in a horseshoe like a rappeller clinging to the side of a mountain. Tall and skinny, Mr. Tipton wore glasses, which made him look older than he was.

"Yes, I need Kaley to come with me to the office for just a moment," Miss Fischer said.

"Ooooh." The muffled commentary rose from the boys around the room. That was one downside to a ten-to-three, guy-to-girl ratio in the class. The guys couldn't be ignored.

Miss Fischer looked at them disapprovingly and placed one hand on her round hip. "You guys should know better than to think that Kaley's in trouble."

It was a minor victory. Kaley knew she wasn't in trouble, but that fact didn't slow her racing heart or cause the beads of sweat to stop forming on her palms. Fear gripped her heart as she imagined who was waiting on the other end of the phone. Her grandfather had undergone a complicated heart surgery earlier in the week and was still in the hospital recovering. She hoped this wasn't the bad news that she had been dreading.

"Yes, Miss Fischer, by all means. Kaley can get the notes from a classmate when she returns," Mr. Tipton said.

Kaley got up from her desk and placed her highlighter inside her textbook to hold her place. As she moved to follow Miss Fischer through the doorway and out into the hallway, she looked at her best friend, Tiffany, in the desk beside her and whispered, "Let me copy your notes when I get back?"

Tiffany nodded and plastered a strained smile across her face. Kaley shared everything with Tiffany, including the details about her grandfather's declining health. The creases in her face and pursed lips gave away the uneasiness she felt for Kaley, as well.

The school office was less than fifty yards away from Mr. Tipton's classroom, but the walk seemed to drag on for a mile as Kaley followed Miss Fischer into the small office. She played every possible scenario over in her head, imagining which of her parents' voices she would hear on the other end of the line. Miss Fischer pointed her to the corded black phone sitting on the edge of her cluttered desk.

"Hello?" Kaley spoke into the receiver, her voice barely a whisper.

"Can you tell me, what is impossible with God?"

It was Coach Middleton.

"What?" Kaley asked, confused.

"Tell me, Kaley. What is impossible with our God?" she repeated.

"Nothing, Coach." And like that, it hit her. Kaley knew what her coach was calling to say before she even uttered the words.

"Kaley, I just got a call from the director of the state tournament. He asked if we would like to accept a bid to play in the first round of the tournament Thursday night," Coach Middleton said.

She continued talking, and while Kaley heard her, she wasn't really listening. Kaley was beautifully broken, the news almost too wonderful to believe, and at a loss for words. Her team was going to state. They had done it. Actually, they hadn't done anything. God had done it, just like in the movie.

"Kaley, are you still there? Can you hear me?" The urgency in Coach Middleton's voice brought Kaley back to reality.

"Yes, sorry, Coach," Kaley squeaked. "I just can't believe it."

"Well, believe it, girly. In two days, you'll be playing in the first round of the state tournament. In the meantime, I need you to let the team know. I've asked Miss Fischer to have all the teachers dismiss any girls' basketball players from fifth period five minutes early. They'll meet you in the chapel in about half an hour. Tell them we'll have a shoot-around practice this afternoon for anyone who can make it," Coach Middleton instructed.

"But Coach," Kaley interrupted. "No one has any of their shoes or shorts or protective braces. We all thought the season was over."

"I've already called your mom. She's planning to meet you at the school after seventh period. She'll bring extra t-shirts and shorts for anyone who needs them," Coach Middleton continued. "I'll meet you guys at Bethlehem around 3:30 this afternoon, okay?"

"Sure, Coach. Oh my goodness, does it get any better than this?"

"With God, it's always better," Coach Middleton said. "He's in the business of the impossible."

"One more question, Coach? What team are we playing?" Kaley asked.

She could hear her coach chuckle on the other end of the line. "The team is from Miracle Academy."

*

Two days later, on Thursday afternoon, Kaley and her teammates huddled around Coach Middleton during the final timeout of their first round game of the state tournament. The large gymnasium was loud, the fans from the opposing schools yelling encouragement to their respective teams.

"All right, ladies. There's two minutes left, and we're down by twelve," Coach Middleton said, her face red as she struggled to be heard over the noise of the crowd. "There's plenty of time for a comeback, but you've got to work together. Focus on the little things. Good passes, smart shots, tough defense."

The buzzer sounded a warning that the timeout was over, and one of the referees walked over to break up the Pineview huddle.

Kaley stretched her hand into the center of the circle. "Okay, ladies. Flames on three. One. Two. Three."

"Flames!" the team cried in unison.

The next two minutes were a blur. Pineview managed to cut the lead to seven but never really took possession of the game. As the final seconds ticked off the clock, Kaley passed the ball to Sophie, whose shot bounced around the rim and dropped off the side. The final buzzer sounded, and Kaley jogged off the court to congratulate her opponents on the win.

After a quick team meeting in the locker room, Kaley stuffed her sweaty socks and shoes into her gym bag and pulled her gray hoodie over her uniform. She stepped out of the locker room and found her dad waiting just outside the door.

"You played a great game, Kales," her dad said, holding his hand out for a fist bump. "I know it didn't end how you were hoping it would. Are you okay?"

Kaley made a fist and touched her knuckles to his. She was tempted to be down because her basketball career had finally come to an end, but taking a deep breath, she said, "Yes, I am okay. At the beginning of the season, I asked God for one impossible thing – a spot in the state tournament. And tonight He gave me that, because He is in the business of the impossible."

20,000 lbs.

Job 42:2 – I know that you can do all things; no plan of yours can be thwarted.

      Caroline's eyes flew open at the strange sound coming from outside the window. It was a noise she had never heard before and was comparable to nothing she knew, a strange mix between a sheep's bleat and a cow's moo. She rubbed her eyes and slowly sat up in bed. A quick glance around the dark bedroom revealed what she expected – the other five girls were still asleep in their bunks.

The sun had not yet risen so the only source of light in the room came from the moon reflecting through the single window across from her bed. The old, rickety fan clicked as it spun in the center of the ceiling.

Caroline pulled her hair up off her neck and quickly tied it back in a ponytail with the thin black rubber band she kept around her wrist. Her hands searched in vain for the sheet that covered her at night before she realized that she had already thrown it off in her sleep. Her shirt was damp with sweat. *I guess that's what happens when you stay in a house that has no air conditioning on a hot summer night,* she thought as she climbed carefully down from her top bunk.

When her feet touched the bedroom's stone floor she was surprised by the coolness of it. Caroline reached up and felt between her mattress and the wooden frame of the bed for her miniature flashlight. Using the small beam of light, she dodged the suitcases and shoes that lay strewn across the floor of the room she shared with the other girls on the mission team and made her way to the small bathroom that connected to the bedroom.

Caroline slowly pushed the wooden door open and shone her light on the windowsill beside the sink. The tarantula that had tormented the girls the night before remained in his place between the two panes of glass, not quite in the bathroom, but certainly not outside where he belonged.

She shuddered before taking her washrag down from where it hung over the rusted shower rod. As she moved to the sink, Caroline kept an eye on the hairy spider the entire way and quickly washed the sweaty dampness from her face and neck. Thinking back to the warning from their training workshops about the bacteria in the water, she was careful not to get any of the potentially hazardous liquid in her mouth. When she had asked God last year for the opportunity to experience His power through new eyes, she had never imagined it would involve spending a week and a half of the summer somewhere so drastically different and removed from her comfort zone as Cayes, Haiti.

Caroline grabbed her Bible and journal from her suitcase and crept out of the bedroom. She wove through the maze of hallways at the Cambry guest house where her mission team was staying during their trip and stepped out into the morning air. While not exactly crisp, the air outside felt much fresher, and even cooler, than the air inside the bedroom.

The guest house was nothing fancy by American standards, but it was a comfortable place to stay. Compared to the living conditions in the rest of Haiti, especially since the terrible earthquake that had destroyed so much of the country just four months before their trip, the guest house was a mansion.

The single-floor structure was made of tan concrete slabs. It was designed in a rough U-shape and had several hallways that doubled back on themselves, making it easy to get lost in the house. Some of the windows had panes, but many had been broken out either during or after the earthquake. The house had two large bedrooms, and several smaller rooms that could be used as makeshift bedrooms if needed. A small kitchen and pantry were tucked away in the interior of the house, and a living room that served as the gathering place for meals and meetings connected the outside and inside of the house.

Carefully avoiding the tree stumps and rubble that surrounded the concrete structure, Caroline walked to the side of the guest house, where a ladder rested against the side of the building and connected the ground to the roof. An animal she couldn't identify greeted the morning somewhere in the distance, but she recognized the sound as the same one that had woken her up earlier.

After she tucked her Bible and journal into the pocket of her baggy athletic shorts, Caroline climbed carefully to the top of the ladder. She stepped onto the flat roof and walked over to where three long planks of wood had been set out as a bench. Checking for spiders and other bugs, she sat gingerly on one of the planks and placed her books on the wood beside her.

Leaning back and looking up into the sky, Caroline gazed at the thousands of stars that dotted the vast blackness, a huge difference from the sky she was used to back home. She smiled. Without the lights of a suburban area, the stars seemed brighter. It made her feel much smaller than she even realized was possible.

Turning her attention from the sky to the rolling hills of the beautiful countryside, Caroline noticed that clusters of sheep and mountain goats dotted the green landscape and trees popped up out of the ground like little people. As she squinted across the field, Caroline made out the form of a Haitian walking along a thin pathway with his dog. Even from a distance, she could see his brown skin, darkened from hours spent under the scorching sun, and a large straw hat sitting atop his head.

    The first rays of the sun were finally starting to peek over the horizon. The spectacular sunrises were the reason Caroline got up so early every morning. More brilliant and colorful than any dawn she had experienced at home, Haitian sunrises were just another one of the things she felt like she was experiencing anew for the very first time.

    Caroline picked up her journal and turned to the next blank page. She held her Bible up and let a pen slide out from between the pages. In the dawn light, she began to write:

> *Here in Haiti the sun rises early and sets late. And one of the best places to revel in this, the beauty of one of God's most breathtaking masterpieces, is on the roof of the Cambry guest house where we're staying while ministering in Cayes, Haiti.*
>
> *I'm up on the rooftop of the guest house. This is by far my favorite place to start the morning. Me and God. So, God, here's what I'm asking You for this morning during our time together on the roof: I'm approaching the throne –*

Your throne of grace – and I'm asking You to work among us (my team and I) in such a way that all we can say, without a shadow of a doubt, "That was God."

"Hey, Caroline! Are you up there? It's almost time for breakfast," a familiar male voice called from somewhere below her. She knew it was her brother.

"Yes, I'm on my way down," she replied as she gathered her books and walked toward the edge of the roof.

*

"Everybody here?" Pastor Dave, the leader of the mission team, asked as he climbed onto the old beat-up school bus. Because he'd been to Haiti several times in the past, Pastor Dave was by far the most qualified for the job. Tall and solidly built, he wore thick glasses and had a full head of wavy gray hair. A grandfather type in his early sixties with a loud laugh that could light up a room, Pastor Dave was fun to be around. Additionally, he was kind and fiercely protective, which made Caroline feel both safe and valued when in his presence.

Caroline looked around at everyone on the bus, mentally checking each teenager off an imaginary list as she looked at the back of his or her head. Her dad and brother sat a few rows in front of her. She nodded, and several teens added a "yes, sir."

"All right. Then let's pray and head for the village," Pastor Dave said. He led the group in a short prayer, thanking God for a safe place to rest and good food for breakfast. He asked for safety in their travels and for energy as the team would build benches for the school and lead a Vacation Bible School with the children in the small rural village in Chantal.

When Pastor Dave finished praying he turned to Titus, one of the Haitian contacts for the mission team, and gave him the all clear to leave. Titus was one of the only men in the village who could speak English. What he knew of the language was limited, but without Titus, the American team would have been unable to communicate with the Haitian people at all. Titus also doubled as the team's tour guide, driving them the hour and a half it took to reach the village each morning and the return trip to the guest house each evening.

Titus was a tall man in his thirties with dark skin blackened even more from his hours working outside under the hot sun. His face was long and his bald head tapered to a point. Jovial by nature, his big smile filled his whole face and revealed a gap between his front teeth.

Titus turned the key in the ignition, and the bus rumbled to life. His loud voice carried back through the bus. "Everybody take you seat an' hold on tight!"

Caroline looked around the worn-out bus and wondered how much longer the vehicle would last. It had lost its air conditioning capability long ago, which probably didn't really matter since most of the windows had been broken out. At one time, the exterior of the bus must have been a solid shade of sunshine yellow, but years in the harsh Haitian climate had caused the paint to peel and allowed the gray metal frame to peek through the paint. Like school buses back home in the States, the interior of the bus had two rows of gray bench seats down the sides, with a narrow walkway between them. The padding in the cushions was almost nonexistent, and there were no seatbelts.

Titus removed his foot from the brake, causing the bus to lurch forward. Caroline grabbed onto the seat in front of her for balance and situated herself in the middle of the bench seat. The team was small enough that no one had to share seats, making the long ride to and from the village a little more pleasant.

Caroline considered the ride ahead of them, the same trek they had made the previous two mornings. They had to wind down the steep mountain road to the narrow streets of Cayes.

On the straightaway that led through the middle of the small, but overpopulated town, Titus usually maxed out the bus's speed at around forty miles per hour as he navigated through the crowded streets. In his attempt to dodge the children, goats, and chickens that ran out into the street and played between the tires, he steered the bus over countless potholes that jarred everyone inside it, bouncing them out of their seats.

Caroline brought herself back to reality and looked out the window to her right as Titus turned the bus in a large circle on the gravel driveway at the top of the mountain. The rocks crunched underneath the heavy weight of the bus as the tires ground them together.

"Hey, Caroline?" Becca asked as she tapped Caroline's shoulder from behind. Becca was fifteen with short, wavy black hair that fell to her shoulders. She tucked her long bangs behind her ears to keep them out of her eyes. Because Becca's family was Korean, her skin had a natural tan year round. She was kind, soft-spoken, and mature for her age.

Caroline turned in the seat to look at the girl three years younger than herself. "Yeah, Becca? What's up?" she asked.

"I was wondering if you would listen to my notes for the Bible story at Vacation Bible School today. I'm a little nervous about speaking to the kids. I just don't want them to miss anything through the translator. I want my words and message to be simple enough that she can convey it to them in a way that is easy to understand."

"Sure, Becca. I'd love to," Caroline said. She perched backwards on her knees so that she could look directly at Becca and hear her quiet voice more easily over the roar of the engine. "What's the topic of the story you're teaching?"

"My message is about the reality of Christ and what He did for all of us on the cross," Becca said and sighed. The weight of what she had to share with the kids made the features of her face look strained and taut. Becca opened her mouth to continue, but before she could say anything else, the bus tires slipped on the loose gravel.

"Hold on, everybody!" Titus yelled from the front of the bus as he struggled against the wheel to keep the vehicle from careening down the steep slope of the mountainside or from crashing headlong into one of the trees that lined the long driveway.

    Caroline quickly flipped back around to face forward and grabbed the seatback in front of her with both hands. Her knuckles turned white as she gripped the worn leather seat with all of her might. Her teammates screamed and gasped as the bus slid out of control down the mountain, but she could barely breathe, much less make any sound. Caroline closed her eyes and waited for the bus to stop.

    Time seemed to stand still until Caroline finally felt the bus stop moving. The sudden braking pushed her forward in the seat, and she opened one eye just enough to see that the bus had stopped on the side of the mountain. It was pointed headfirst down the steep slope, and somehow it had miraculously halted inches away from slamming head-on with a large tree.

    Caroline didn't move for fear that even the smallest action would dislodge the bus from its place on the slope and cause it to slide into the tree. She tried to calm her racing heart by taking slow deep breaths through her nose.

    Caroline looked around the bus at the rest of her teammates. Each coped with the stress of the situation in his or her own way. Her dad turned around in his seat, allowing his gaze to meet her own. He raised an eyebrow as if asking if she was okay. Caroline nodded and smiled when her brother offered her a thumbs-up. Melanie, a tall thin girl with long brown hair, sat in the seat directly across from Caroline. Melanie's eyes were closed, her fists clenched in her lap. Pastor Dave sat ahead of her. Caroline saw his mouth moving and surmised that he was whispering prayers.

When Caroline glanced over her shoulder at Becca, she was met by the younger girl's large, round eyes staring back at her. Caroline offered the frightened girl a small smile, hoping to reassure her. Jordan sat on the other side of the center aisle and stared out at the crowd around the bus.

Caroline turned her attention to the paneless window on her side of the bus and scooted closer to it for a better view. The tires had slid off of the gravel pathway leading down the mountain and rested on the green grass of the hillside. A small group of men, women, and children gathered several yards away from the bus. Caroline couldn't understand what they were saying, but their furtive glances and gestures toward the bus revealed that they were excited and concerned.

Several children huddled up next to the fence that ran along the property line. They waved to Caroline. She recognized them from the orphanage at the bottom of the mountain and waved back. Despite the seriousness of the situation, she caught herself smiling at the memory of the midnight dance party she and her team had chaperoned in the small stone orphanage the first night they arrived in Haiti.

Caroline refocused her attention from the children to the interior of the bus. Several of her teammates talked quietly among themselves. Caroline heard snatches of their conversation. At the front of the bus, Pastor Dave, Titus, and her dad stood in a small triangle, their brows furrowed. They were too far away from where she sat to hear what they were saying, but she knew they were discussing what to do with the bus now.

While she watched, Titus and her dad nodded and stepped back to make a path for Pastor Dave to move toward the back of the bus where the teenagers were waiting.

"Okay, everyone. May I have your attention, please," Pastor Dave's deep voice boomed.

All talking stopped, and each of the teenagers turned his full attention to the pastor.

"We've talked it over," Pastor Dave said as he motioned to the other two men standing just behind him, "and we think it would be best to get everyone off the bus before we try to do anything else. If you'll make your way quickly and carefully to the front of the bus, we'll help you down. Once you're outside, step away from the bus until we've decided what our next course of action will be."

The teenagers waited for Pastor Dave to continue, but when he didn't say anything else, they realized he was finished and carefully made their way to the front of the vehicle. Caroline sat in one of the back two rows so she was one of the last off the bus. When she reached the steps, her dad was waiting on the sloped ground and offered her his hand. He wore a white t-shirt and a floppy tan hat that kept the sun off his face and neck. He wasn't a tall man, but he was deceptively strong.

"You okay?" he asked Caroline as she stepped down and joined him on the hill.

Caroline looked up at her hero, who stood only a few inches taller than she did, and nodded. "Yes, sir. That was just a little unexpected," she said and laughed hesitantly. "Um, Dad?"

"Yes, dear?"

"We're not going anywhere anytime soon, are we? Like, the bus is really stuck?"

Her dad removed his hat and ran a hand through his thick, brown hair. "We're going to do our best, but the bus itself easily weighs upwards of twenty tons. It would take a miracle for a handful of men to move the bus on flat ground, much less angled down a steep incline."

Caroline nodded and quietly joined the other girls on the team where they stood surrounded by a group of children from the orphanage. Caroline set her backpack on the ground.

Levi, a little boy she'd met during her first night in Haiti, came up beside her. He pointed first to her backpack and then to himself. Caroline immediately understood. She nodded and helped him slip the straps over his shoulders. Levi tucked his small hand into hers as he looked up at her and flashed a smile that covered his entire face.

From a distance, Caroline and Levi, the mission team, and the other orphans watched Titus climb back into the bus and crank the engine. Its front end had fallen into the ditch on the side of the guest house driveway. After several attempts to back the bus out of the ditch, Caroline realized that the bus wouldn't be going anywhere anytime soon. *Why would you let this happen, God? You know we're not strong enough to move a bus. We had an important message to share with the kids today, but now they won't even get a chance to hear it,* Caroline prayed.

Titus appeared in the doorway of the bus and waved Pastor Dave over. They talked for a minute before Pastor Dave walked over to the guys on the team, and Titus addressed several of the men standing around watching. They all nodded and immediately started moving toward the front of the bus. The men arranged themselves around the hood, carving out footholds in the hard-packed dirt on the side of the mountain. While they pushed against the bus, Titus worked the gas pedal. With tires spinning and emitting smoke, the bus moved, but only backed up centimeters before rolling back into the ditch.

As the minutes passed, more curious orphans cautiously approached the scene and walked up to Caroline and the girls. They grabbed onto the girls' hands and eagerly waited to see what would happen next. While the men added wooden beams underneath the back tires for traction and wedged rocks underneath the rubber as the bus moved back inches, the girls prayed quietly among themselves for a miracle.

While Becca was voicing her request aloud, Caroline thought about what she had written in her journal that morning on the rooftop:

> *The life of a believer is a battlefield, and spiritual warfare is a very real thing. But I can't say we weren't warned. Take, for example,*

John 16:33. As some of His last words to His disciples, Jesus said, "In this world you will have trouble. But take heart! I have overcome the world."

If you pay close attention to the wording from that verse, you'll notice that Jesus didn't say, "If you happen to experience a little bit of trouble here or there" or "There might occasionally be a roadblock that pops up unexpectedly." Rather, He said, "You WILL have trouble."

The implication, then, is clearly not IF but WHEN. Even as Christians, or maybe especially as Christians, we are not exempt from the trials and tribulations of this world. We are still human beings, complete with a sinful nature, living in the wake of the consequences of The Fall. My favorite part of the verse in John 16, however, is that last phrase – the incredible promise that Christ's victory leaves no reason to fear.

Caroline hadn't known, and certainly hadn't imagined, that the trouble she read about by the light of the sunrise would come so quickly or so drastically.

Pastor Dave walked over to the circle of girls and laid his hands on Caroline's shoulders. "Hey, ladies, I don't mean to interrupt, but do you think that you could give us a hand with the bus?"

The girls looked up at Pastor Dave and nodded, excited to be needed in the pressing situation.

"Great. We need y'all to hop back on the bus. We're thinking that maybe the added weight will increase the traction of the wheels," Pastor Dave said and motioned over his shoulder with his thumb. "Also, how about taking several of the kids with you," he added with a twinkle in his eye.

Smiles broke out on all six of the girls' faces as they pulled the orphans with them toward the bus. The kids looked up at the girls, confused.

Caroline pointed from Levi to the bus, and his eyes grew wide in excitement. He pointed from himself to the bus. When Caroline nodded, he took off toward the bus, dragging her along behind him. *He's probably never been in any type of vehicle before,* Caroline thought as she fought back tears.

The girls helped the little orphan boys onto the bus before climbing in behind them. They moved everyone to the same side of the bus so that their weight would push down on the back right tire that was stuck in the ditch. Then, with the men pushing, the girls praying, and the orphans talking and laughing and bouncing up and down on the seats, Titus revved the engine and tried again…

And again…

And again…

Nothing.

On the last try, with a scenario identical to the previous attempts, the bus crept backward up the steep embankment, out of the ditch, and away from the tree. The orphans shouted even louder, the men stood back from the bus and wiped the sweat from their brows, and the girls looked at each other in disbelief.

Titus guided the bus down the steep embankment and parked it on the flat ground in front of the orphanage. Everybody jumped off the bus and ran up the hill to where the men talked and laughed.

Caroline jogged over to her dad. "Oh my gosh! Did you see that? Y'all just pushed a bus up a mountain! How is that even possible?" The questions flooded out of her mouth faster than her dad could answer.

Caroline's dad put his hand on her shoulder to calm her and laughed. He was still panting from the exertion of the past half hour. "It's not possible," he said simply.

Caroline looked at him, her face scrunched up in question. "What do you mean?"

"I mean it's impossible. Like I told you earlier, there literally is no conceivable way that seven men and three teenagers could push a bus filled with more than twenty orphans backward up a hill. That's more than twenty thousand pounds up an incline. It just isn't possible," he said.

Caroline shook her head in wonder. She looked over to where Pastor Dave was shaking hands and slapping the backs of the men who had helped rescue the bus. When he had thanked everyone, Pastor Dave called the team over. The ten teenagers, Titus, and Caroline's dad circled up around Pastor Dave and waited to hear what he would say.

Pastor Dave took a deep breath. "Well, guys. What you just experienced was a miracle. There is no other explanation," he said. He ran his hand through his hair and shook his head as if he still couldn't grasp what had just happened. He told the group that they would still be headed to the village of Chantal where they would continue their work on the schoolhouse as well as leading Vacation Bible School with the kids.

That night Caroline climbed into bed, exhausted and in awe. Before she turned the lights out for the night, she pulled out her journal and jotted down some thoughts from the day:

> *You know what the funny thing is, though? We didn't do anything differently on that final attempt. Does it seem even remotely possible that a few men and a couple of teenagers could possess the strength to push a twenty thousand pound bus out of a ditch and up the side of a mountain? I think not.*
>
> *But, you see, that's the miracle of our weakness. I love what Paul says in 2 Corinthians 12:9-10. "'My grace is sufficient for you, for my power is made perfect in weakness.' Therefore I will boast all the more gladly about my weaknesses, so that Christ's power*

may rest on me. That is why, for Christ's sake, I delight in weaknesses, in insults, in hardships, in persecutions, in difficulties. For when I am weak, then I am strong."

Today we were weak. Very weak. But we serve a strong God. A God of angel armies. Sometimes we may be granted the opportunity to entertain angels.

And sometimes, they might just entertain us.

Chloe

Hebrews 13:2 – Do not forget to entertain strangers, for by doing so some people have entertained angels without knowing it.

"Okay, Caleb. Are you ready?" Trista turned to her brother as they stood together on the front porch of their neighbor's house.

Caleb nodded. He knocked on the door and took a step back.

"And remember, it's your turn to do the talking," Trista said.

At thirteen, Trista was two years older than her brother. Generally more outgoing, she usually jumped at the opportunity to talk. However, fundraising door-to-door in her neighborhood brought out her shy side. For that reason, she and her brother often took turns soliciting funds from the families in the neighborhood.

Caleb looked at her, his brow furrowed. "No it's not! I can't talk this time." He leaned closer to her and whispered, "This is the scary lady's house."

Trista rolled her eyes and opened her mouth to respond when the door opened to reveal a short elderly lady in a floral robe and light pink bedroom slippers. Mrs. Avery wore glasses and had white hair that curled close to her head.

Trista looked to her brother, expecting him to talk. When her gaze was met by his startled, bright blue eyes, she realized that wasn't going to happen.

"Uh, good evening, Mrs. Avery. How are you?" The words rushed out of Trista's mouth.

"I'm fine, dear. Is there something I can do for you? I was just about to turn in for the night," the old lady said.

"We're sorry to bother you," Trista said, motioning to her brother. "Caleb and I are looking for sponsors for the Aiken Pregnancy Care Center's Lifewalk. As in previous years, we'll be walking two miles around the track at Four Acres Park. The Lifewalk is next Saturday morning, and all donations are tax-deductible. The money will be given to young moms who need help caring for their babies. We were wondering if you'd like to make a donation?"

Mrs. Avery smiled, revealing teeth that had grown crooked and yellowed with age. "You're doing that walk again, huh? Good for you. Let me go see if I have any cash in my purse. Would you like to come inside?"

"It's okay. We'll wait here," Trista said.

Mrs. Avery left the door open and disappeared into the house.

Trista looked over her shoulder to where her parents were waiting beside the road. She gave them a quick thumbs-up and saw them smile back. This was the same ritual they engaged in each fall: her parents would walk the neighborhood with her and Caleb each night after dinner while the kids went door-to-door asking for donations for the young couples the pregnancy center helped.

"I think I'm gonna go wait with Mom and Dad," Caleb said as he edged toward the porch steps.

"Oh no you're not," Trista said. She grabbed the sleeve of his jacket and pulled him back toward the door. "I'm not doing this alone. Besides, she wasn't even that scary this time."

"I don't know what you were looking at. Didn't you see her teeth?" Caleb quipped.

Trista jabbed her brother in the side with her elbow as Mrs. Avery reappeared in the doorway. She held a five-dollar bill in each hand.

"I know it's not much, but it's all I have with me," she said. She handed one bill to Trista. "Here's one for you."

"Thank you, Mrs. Avery," Trista said.

"And here's one for you, young man." Mrs. Avery held the second bill out to Caleb, who reached tentatively for it.

"Thank you, Mrs. Avery," he said, his voice cracking.

"You're quite welcome. Both of you. Isn't it a little late for y'all to be out alone?" Mrs. Avery asked.

"Oh, we're not alone. Our parents are over there," Trista said, pointing to the road.

Mrs. Avery stuck her head out the door and waved to the couple. "Tell them it was good to see them. And thank you for stopping by. It's refreshing to see young people who want to make a positive difference in the community. You made this old woman's night," Mrs. Avery said with a wink.

Trista smiled at the woman. "Thank you for the donation. We really appreciate it," she said. "Have a good night. Bye, Mrs. Avery."

*

Five days later, Trista and Caleb met several friends at Four Acres for the Lifewalk. The sky was overcast and the air was cool, but the storms were expected to hold off until later in the afternoon. Trista was relieved that the weather would not affect the walk. For as long as she could remember, her family had always been involved in the Lifewalk. When she and Caleb were too little to complete the walk themselves, her mom had pushed them the two miles in a stroller. In more recent years, Trista had grown to look forward to the new t-shirts with bright designs and the carnival games and bake sales that took place when the walk was finished.

"Hey, Allie! How are you?" Trista called as she ran up to her best friend and enveloped her in a big hug. Allie and her mom had participated in the Lifewalk almost as long as Trista's family.

"I'm good. How are you?" Allie asked, her voice muffled against Trista's hoodie.

"I'm good, too. Have you already turned in your money?" Trista asked.

Allie shook her head. "No, I just got here. Have you?"

"Nope. Caleb and I were about to go get in line. You can join us if you'd like," Trista said.

The trio walked over the registration line where they met Caleb's friend, Kyle. Kyle and Caleb were born just a day apart and had been friends since before they could remember. Unlike Caleb, who was shy, Kyle took pride in being the life of the party. Trista often wondered if his extroverted tendencies were more the result of growing up with three brothers or the fact that he was a ginger.

Allie and Trista walked the two laps around the track together, talking and laughing the whole way. Caleb and Kyle ran ahead of them, so that they could get in line for the carnival games before all of the good prizes were given out. The girls found the guys after they had finished their two miles and watched them compete in balloon darts and participate in a cakewalk before they were interrupted by a voice booming through a set of loudspeakers.

Trista looked up to see Mrs. Wilson, the Center's director, standing on top of a table underneath the covered picnic area. With one hand she held a bullhorn in front of her face. Her other hand clutched a piece of paper.

"Good morning. I think everyone has finished the walk, so if you all could make your way toward the picnic area, we're ready to announce the winners in each category and give away some prizes!"

"Come on, Caleb. It's time for prizes," Trista called to her brother who was too busy aiming a dart at a wooden board filled with balloons to focus on the announcement.

Caleb threw the dart and popped a blue balloon. "Yes!" he exclaimed, high-fiving Kyle and grabbing a handful of candy from the prize bucket. "I'm coming, Trista," he cried as he started toward her.

The four kids worked their way to the front of the crowd where they waited for Mrs. Wilson to announce the money-amount winners in each of the age categories. Mrs. Wilson started with the youngest age group and worked her way up. When she got to the ten- to fifteen-year-olds, Trista held her breath. Beside her, Caleb closed his eyes and crossed his fingers, waiting for the winner's name to be announced.

"The third place winner in the fifteen and under category is... Caleb Barnwell!"

Caleb pumped his fists and smiled at his sister as he ran to where Mrs. Wilson stood at the picnic table holding his goody bag. He took it from her. Racing back to his spot in the crowd, Caleb immediately started rummaging through his prize.

"The second place prize in the fifteen and under category is... Allie Montgomery!"

Trista gave Allie a quick hug and clapped with the crowd as her friend skipped up to the table and received her bag of gifts.

"This year, the first place prize in the fifteen and under category is a brand new bike. The winner of this category raised over one thousand dollars for the center this year. So without further ado, first place is awarded to Trista Barnwell!"

Caleb turned around and gave his sister a high-five. "I knew it was gonna be you," he said, a big grin plastered across his face.

Allie wrapped an arm around Trista's shoulders and gave her a quick squeeze. "Great job, friend! One thousand dollars? That's amazing!"

Trista smiled and bit her lip as she walked to the picnic table where Mrs. Wilson was waiting to present her with the bike. She thought about all the hours she had spent writing letters to family who lived far away, the phone calls she had made to her parents' friends, and the miles she had walked through several neighborhoods in the city. She had worked hard to raise that thousand dollars, and she was proud of her success. After she hugged Mrs. Wilson, the woman held the handlebars out for Trista to take.

Trista stood on her tiptoes and cupped her hand around her mouth as she pulled Mrs. Wilson's shoulder down so she could whisper in her ear. She watched as the expression on the woman's face changed from joy to confusion to awe.

"Are you sure that's what you want?" Mrs. Wilson asked.

Trista nodded. "Yes, ma'am. I'm positive."

Clearing her throat and drawing Trista to her side so the girl could face the crowd, Mrs. Wilson spoke into the microphone again. "It looks like there's been a little twist this year. Trista just informed me that she would like to give up her right to the bike so that the center can return it and keep the money or use it for future fundraising endeavors."

The crowd broke out in spontaneous applause, shouting praise and encouragement for the girl. Trista felt her face grow hot and quickly rejoined her friends in the crowd where she was smothered with hugs and peppered with questions.

Caleb looked at his older sister, eyes wide with admiration. "Wow, Trista, that was so nice of you. Didn't you want the bike, though?"

Trista smiled at her brother. "A part of me did. That bike was nice! But I couldn't help thinking about how I already have a bike that works, and I figured the Center probably needs the money more than I need another bike. That money could help a lot of people."

Caleb nodded slowly. He reached into his prize bag and held out a handful of miniature chocolate bars. "Here. We can share my prize. I think you'll probably enjoy this chocolate more than I would anyway. It has nuts in it."

*

"Before we're dismissed, one young lady has a special message she wants to share with us this morning. Trista, it's all yours," Pastor

Hartford said as he held out his hand and helped her up the steps to the large wooden pulpit.

Pastor Hartford was a tall man with broad shoulders from his college days as a football player at the University of Miami. His dark brown hair was thinning as he worked his way through his forties.

"Thanks, Pastor Hartford," Trista whispered as she gave him a quick hug. She spread her notes out on the pulpit and adjusted the microphone. *You're okay, Trista. These people are like family, and you've been asking them for Lifewalk donations since you were ten. You can do this.* Inspired by her self-proclaimed pep talk, Trista drew a quick breath and dove into the short speech she had prepared.

"Good morning, everyone. Many of you know me, but for those of you who don't, my name is Trista Barnwell. I'm twenty-one years old and am a junior at the University of South Carolina Aiken. Dry Branch Baptist has been my home since I was in the first grade, and today I want to share with you about another ministry that, thanks to my mom's influence when I was just a child, I hold close to my heart.

"The Aiken Pregnancy Care Center's Lifewalk is quickly approaching and will be held at Four Acres as it has in previous years. This is the fifteenth Lifewalk that I have participated in, and I want to give you all the opportunity to be a blessing to the Center as it influences the lives of countless women, both young and old, in our community.

"The APCC is a non-profit, non-denominational ministry that provides expectant women with information about their options, encouragement to choose life for their unborn child, and counsel for those dealing with the effects of an abortion. They also offer classes for new mothers and stock diapers, baby clothes, and formula at greatly discounted prices.

"The annual Lifewalk is the Center's primary source of income, and all donations are tax deductible. What am I asking you today? First, if you would like to make a monetary donation, you can do so before you leave church. Following the service, I will be in the lobby and can answer questions and accept cash or checks made out to APCC. If you don't feel led to give, perhaps you would like to take a visible stand for the unborn by coming out to walk next Saturday morning. But most importantly, today I am asking you to pray. These unborn children can't speak for themselves; they need someone to speak on their behalf. Would you join with me in giving them a voice?

"Thank you."

As the sanctuary broke out into applause, Trista refolded her notes and stepped down from the pulpit, pausing by the pew where her family sat. "I'm going to wait out back in case anyone wants to donate today," she whispered in her mother's ear before she continued out the back doors of the sanctuary to the lobby.

A few minutes later, the back doors opened and people dressed in fancy clothes poured out the doors toward the parking lot. Trista stood off to one side of the lobby, waiting to see if anyone would bring donations for her cause. To her surprise, a line quickly formed in front of her as several of the older couples in the church, many of whom had been her Sunday school teachers or choir directors, stopped to give her money.

"We are so proud of you," Mrs. Leslie said. Daniel and Leslie Chandler were in their seventies and had been Trista's third grade Sunday school teachers. They still stopped her in the hallway every time they saw her at church to ask how she was doing. Mr. Daniel patted Trista on the back while his wife gave her a big hug and kiss on the cheek, leaving some of her bright red lipstick behind.

"Thank you both so much," Trista said. "I really appreciate your support. I know that the Center will, too."

Mr. Daniel looked over his shoulder. "Leslie, we need to let her go. There are quite a few people waiting to talk with Trista. We don't want to keep them waiting."

"Oh, of course," Mrs. Leslie said. "Good luck, Trista. Let us know how the walk goes, okay? We'd love to hear about it."

"Yes, ma'am. I'll do that," Trista said as she waved goodbye to the couple.

When the line had disappeared twenty minutes later, Trista's parents joined her by the welcome desk in the spacious lobby.

"Looked like you had quite the support group today," her dad said.

Trista couldn't repress the grin that spread across her face. "It was so overwhelming – more than I could have imagined."

"How much do you think you raised today?" her mom asked, hooking her arm through her daughter's as they walked toward the car.

"I'm not exactly sure, but I'd guess somewhere between five and seven hundred dollars," Trista estimated.

As they reached the doors leading to the parking lot, Trista heard a voice behind her. "Excuse me? Are you the girl who gave that wonderful speech at the end of the service?"

Trista turned around, expecting to be greeted by someone she knew. Instead, she found herself face-to-face with a woman she had never seen before.

"Uh, yes, ma'am, I am. My name is Trista." She held out her hand to the woman. "Is there something I can do for you?"

The woman reached out and shook Trista's hand but did not offer a name. The woman had long, strawberry blond hair that was collected into a frizzy braid down her back. Her wrinkled face showed signs of sun damage, making her appear older than she likely was. The woman spoke with a northern accent and her eyes danced behind big, round glasses when she talked.

"Well, yes. I think there might be. I was wondering if there are other needs that the Center might have on the day of the walk?" the lady asked.

Trista frowned and cocked her head. "I'm not sure I understand," she said.

"Are there any ways I could help on the day of the walk, besides just walking? Maybe I could bring some cookies or water for the walkers?" the lady suggested.

"That's so nice of you to offer," Trista said. She thought for a moment. "I'm sure those things would be appreciated, but I think the ladies who run the Center would be able to tell you exactly what their needs are on the day of the Lifewalk. Perhaps you could call them and ask?"

"Okay, I can do that. I just thought it might be nice to have some food and drinks out there for the walkers," the lady said.

"I think you're right. I don't have the phone number for the Center, but it's in the phone book under Aiken Pregnancy Care Center," Trista said as she turned to leave.

"Oh, one more thing," the lady said.

Trista stopped and looked at the woman. "Yes?"

"You said you walk two miles and that the walk starts at nine in the morning, is that right?"

"Yes, ma'am. Twice around the mile track at the park, and the walk starts at nine," Trista confirmed.

"I'd also like to make a donation to the Center on your behalf." The lady squinted her eyes shut as if thinking hard. "How about this – I'll donate one hundred dollars per lap for every mile you walk above and beyond the required two laps," she said.

Trista's eyes grew wide and her mouth dropped open. "You'll give me one hundred dollars per extra mile?" she asked incredulously.

"Yes, but there's a catch," the woman said. "You only have until one o'clock in the afternoon."

Trista considered the woman's words. "Can I run them? Or the deal is that I walk all of them?"

"You can cover the ground however you would like, but only the miles completed before one will count," the woman said. "Keep track and let me know the total next week here at church."

"Okay, yes. Absolutely. Thank you so much," Trista said.

"See you next week," the woman said as she turned around and walked back toward the sanctuary.

Trista hurried outside to where her parents were waiting at the car.

"Who was that?" her mother asked. "And what was that all about?"

"I've never met her. I actually don't think I've even seen her before, either. But you'll never believe what she offered," Trista said excitedly.

"What?" her mom asked.

"She's going to donate one hundred dollars for every mile after the first two that I walk on Saturday," Trista said. "Well, at least however many I can complete before one o'clock."

"Wow! That's incredible," her mom said. "What did you say the lady's name was?"

Trista hesitated. "I didn't." She paused and furrowed her brow as she replayed the encounter in her head. "She didn't tell me. I introduced myself and shook her hand, but she never gave me her name."

"Then how are you supposed to collect the donation from her?" Trista's mom asked.

"She said to find her at church next week," Trista said. "I guess I just have to look for her."

Her mother raised her eyebrows, skepticism coloring her facial features. "I hope she keeps her end of this, sweetheart, because I know that you will."

*

"So did you ever find the lady who offered you the huge donation?" Carly asked as she tucked a strand of her curly, dark red hair behind her ear.

Trista shook her head as she put two pieces of bacon on her plate next to the spoonful of scrambled eggs and worked her way down the rest of the breakfast buffet line. She took a cup of apple juice from the table and followed Carly to a small table on the other side of the Sunday school room.

Carly and Trista rarely spent time together outside of church functions due to very different personalities and interests. While Trista was athletic, Carly preferred shopping and fashion. Trista didn't care to spend time or money on her hair, but Carly dyed hers a new color every other month.

"So she just like, never showed back up?" Carly asked. She tucked her wavy red hair behind her ear and took a bite of a glazed donut.

"Unfortunately not," Trista said, taking a sip of her juice. "I've looked for her every week since the walk, but that was three weeks ago. I guess it was just too good to be true."

"Surely someone knows her," Carly said absentmindedly. "Have you asked around here at church?"

"Not really," Trista admitted. "The problem is that I don't know anything about her. She didn't even tell me her name."

"That's so strange," Carly said.

"Trista? Someone's here to see you," the Sunday school teacher called from the other side of the room.

Confused, Trista stood and walked to the door where she found the mystery woman waiting for her.

"Hi, Trista. Someone downstairs told me I might find you here. Did you do it?" the woman asked.

"Hi. I've been looking all over for you. Yes, I did," Trista stammered.

"How many miles did you walk?"

"I walked twelve total – ten extra after the first two," Trista said.

"Wow. That's great. Okay, so ten extra miles at one hundred dollars a mile. That'd be one thousand dollars, right?" the woman asked.

Trista nodded. "Yes, ma'am." Eight years ago it had taken Trista the better part of three months to raise one thousand dollars for the Lifewalk. It was hard to believe that this woman was going to single-handedly donate that same amount, all because Trista had walked an extra ten miles.

"I don't have the money with me because I didn't know how much it would be, but I'll bring it to you next week. You'll be here again?" the woman asked.

"Yes, ma'am. I'm here each week," Trista said.

"Okay, see you then," the lady said and walked down the stairs leaving Trista staring after her.

"Was that her?" Carly asked excitedly when Trista returned to her seat still stunned.

"Yeah, it was her," Trista said, dumbfounded.

"What'd she say?" Carly asked.

"She wanted to know how many miles I'd walked and said she'd bring the money next week." Trista relayed the information and shook her head.

"That's awesome! I can't believe she came back," Carly said.

"Me neither. I hope it's not too good to be true."

*

Two weeks later, Trista was back in the college Sunday school class. The mystery donor had not stopped by the previous week, causing Trista to give up the idea that she would ever see the promised donation.

"All right, guys. Everybody pull up a chair. Let's go ahead and get started this morning," Trista's teacher, Coach Day, said.

A tall, thin balding man, Coach Day taught history at the local high school and was the school's former baseball coach. Retired from coaching, he now spent his time investing in the lives of the kids at church.

Trista looked around the room for an empty chair and found a seat a few feet from the door. She sat down next to Carly and turned her attention to Coach Day. As he started the day's lesson, movement in the hallway outside the door caught Trista's attention.

Carly elbowed her. "Oh my gosh. That's your mystery woman, isn't it?"

Trista nodded, unable to speak.

The woman stood outside the hallway and motioned for Trista to join her. Trista stood silently and slipped out the door to meet the woman. She felt Carly's eyes on her from behind.

"I missed you last week, but I wanted to be sure I caught you today," the woman said.

Unable to find words, Trista simply nodded.

"I believe this is what I owe you," the woman said as she handed Trista a white business envelope. "Go ahead. You can open it."

Trista flipped open the top flap and looked inside. She counted ten one hundred dollar bills. *This will help so many people.* As she tucked the flap back inside the body of the envelope, Trista thought of her mom. She had always encouraged Trista to serve others and to try to make a difference. This money would make a huge difference. Her mother would be so proud.

"Thank you," Trista whispered. "This means so much – to me and to the Center."

"No, thank you, darling," the woman said. "What you're doing is an encouragement to us old folks. We all need to act on our convictions. It's refreshing to see the passion of your generation."

Trista smiled, speechless again.

"Well, I better let you get back to class," the woman said as she motioned toward the door and turned to leave.

"Wait!" Trista said. "I didn't catch your name."

The woman smiled, her eyes twinkling mischievously. "Oh, forgive me. I'm Chloe."

Trista held out her hand for the woman to take. "It's nice to meet you, Ms. Chloe, and thank you again. I'm sure I'll see you around," Trista said.

*

The next morning, Trista took the cash by the Center. When she was asked whom it was from, all she could offer was a first name. Chloe. The woman had given her cash, so no identifying last name or address was present like it would be on a check.

Over the following weeks and months, Trista searched for the woman every Sunday. She described the woman's appearance to church members and asked if they knew a woman named Chloe, but no one did.

One Sunday afternoon four months after the Lifewalk, Trista found her mom in the kitchen baking cookies for the local prison ministry. Trista grabbed a warm cookie from the tray and perched on the marble counter. She let her head fall back against the wooden cabinet behind her with a thump.

Between placing globs of cookie dough on the cookie sheet, Trista's mom, Paige, glanced over her shoulder. "Is everything okay, honey?"

Trista nodded. She finished chewing the cookie and said, "Yes, ma'am. I'm just a little frustrated, I guess."

"Would you like to talk about it?" Paige asked.

Trista let out a long sigh. "You already know what it's about. Ever since Chloe found me in Sunday school and gave me the one thousand dollars, I've looked for her everywhere."

"Maybe you should talk to Pastor Hartford. If anyone knows her, my bet is that it would be him."

"I already talked to him," Trista said sheepishly. She hopped down from the counter and took another cookie.

"You did?" Paige stopped scooping cookie dough and looked at her daughter. "How did that go?"

"It was fine. He tried to be helpful, but it didn't really work out. I had already looked through the directory, but he insisted on double-checking. Then he looked through the church's past five years of visitor records. Only two 'Chloe's were listed. One was in middle school and the other was a year and a half old," Trista said.

Paige set the spoon she was using inside the bowl with the remaining cookie dough and wiped her hands on her apron. She tucked a stray piece of her light brown hair behind her ear before placing her hands on Trista's shoulders. "Honey, why are you so intent on finding her?"

Trista opened her mouth to speak, but before any words came out, she stopped. "You know, I'm not really sure." She paused. "Is it wrong that I want to know?"

Paige tilted her head, and Trista knew she was considering her next words carefully. Finally she spoke. "No. I don't think it's wrong to wonder or to be curious," Paige said. She released Trista's shoulders and crossed her arms. "But I do think that some things are more special and hold more meaning when they're not fully known or understood."

"You mean like, if I knew exactly who she was, maybe it would take some of the wonder away?" Trista asked.

Her mother smiled and nodded. "That's exactly what I mean. For all you know, your friend Chloe was just passing through."

Right then, Trista decided it would be okay if she never saw the woman again. *After all,* she concluded, *angels don't need last names.*

Sticky Notes

Hebrews 14:6 – Let us then approach the throne of grace with confidence so that we may receive mercy and find grace to help us in our time of need.

  Isabella pulled her black Mazda 3 into a parking spot and turned off the ignition. She checked the clock on the dash. 5:56. *I've got four minutes to find this class.* She reached behind the driver's seat and groped for her backpack. When she couldn't feel it, Isabella turned around and slid her body through the narrow opening that separated the two front seats. The bag's contents were spread across the back seat and spilled into the floorboard. Isabella huffed, realizing there was no way she could grab everything from her perch in the front of the car.

"For real?" she muttered under her breath.

Isabella clambered out of the car, hitting her head on the doorframe when she stood too quickly.

"Oh my gosh! Could this day get any worse?" Isabella screamed.

She looked around the parking lot. Two rows over, a tall, thin guy with dark brown hair stared at her from where he stood by the open trunk of his car. When he realized she saw him, he quickly slammed the trunk closed, swung his backpack over his shoulder, and hurried across the parking lot toward the big brick science building.

"That's right, run along. There's nothing to see here," Isabella muttered under her breath as she opened the back seat of her car.

The contents of her backpack lay across the carpeted floorboard, mixed with a collection of candy wrappers and empty soda bottles. Isabella brushed her short red hair out of her eyes and bent over the mess. She scooped her textbooks, binders, and a few pencils into her arms and threw them into her backpack.

Threading her arms through the straps of her backpack, she slammed the door and straightened the light blue tank top that hugged her slender frame. She pulled her skinny jeans up on her hips and ran across the parking lot toward the science building.

Isabella threw her weight into the big double doors at the entrance to the massive brick building. She walked quickly down the gray cement hallway, peering in the open doors she passed in her quest to locate the room where her biology lab was meeting. Her shoes clicked against the speckled tiles that lined the floor. When she reached the end of the hallway, Isabella stopped by a classroom doorway and set her backpack on the ground. Scrounging through the papers she had stuffed in her bag, she grabbed her course schedule and checked the room assignment. Lab 203. The number on the paper matched the sign on the door.

Halfway down the hall, a professor stepped out of his office and locked the door behind him. His dark brown hair stood on end and a pair of glasses rested on top of his head. A leather satchel hung across his body, and his untucked shirttail hung down over his khaki pants. As he started in her direction, Isabella ducked into the crowded classroom and scanned the rows of tables for an empty seat. Her line of sight naturally gravitated to the back of the classroom, but the furthest row was already crammed with bodies. *Glad to see I'm not the only one who enjoys mid-class naps,* Isabella thought. After browsing the rest of the room, she realized the only empty seat was in the front row of tables, a zone she had always avoided because it belonged to the studious, over-achieving population of students. In the first three semesters of her college experience, she had made a point of avoiding the front row, and until now, she had been successful.

Isabella looked at her tablemates, sizing them up. To her right, a girl slouched in the chair with her head down. Her long black hair spilled from the hood of the sweatshirt that was pulled over her head. The girl had not looked up since Isabella entered the room.

Isabella looked to her right and was greeted by a friendly smile.

"Hey, I'm Hunter. You're the girl from the parking lot?"

Isabella's face grew hot. She pasted a smile on her face and nervously tucked her hair behind her ears.

"That was me. It's been a long day," she murmured, laughing to hide her embarrassment.

"Don't feel bad. We all have days like that. What did you say your name was?" Hunter asked.

"I didn't. I'm Isabella," she said as she held out her hand.

"It's nice to meet you, Isabella," he said.

"It's nice to meet you, too. You said Hunter, right? I'm not very good with names," she apologized.

"Not a problem. I'm sure I'll be seeing you again. I'll be sure to remind you," Hunter said.

A short man with glasses and bushy white hair appeared at the doorway. He held a Big Gulp Styrofoam cup in one hand and had a stack of books tucked under his other arm.

"Is this Biology 203?" he asked. His accent sounded part Greek, part sandpaper.

Hunter nodded. "Yes, sir, the one and only. Welcome to class."

Isabella looked at Hunter, her mouth gaping in disbelief. "You just welcomed the professor to class? Are you kidding me?" she whispered.

Hunter winked. "You can never start making friends with your professor too soon."

The man stepped into the room. Looking at Hunter, he said, "Thank you for the warm welcome, Mr.?"

"Waters. Hunter Waters."

"I've got my eye on you, Mr. Waters," the professor said.

He set his cup carefully on the table at the front of the room and dropped the books on the hard black surface with a thud.

At least he has his priorities in line, Isabella thought.

"Good evening, class. Let me be the first to welcome you to Biology 203. Unless, of course, Mr. Waters already beat me to it."

A few students chuckled and murmured comments under their breath to their neighbors.

"My name is Carl Jenkins. I have a Ph.D. in biological science from John Hopkins University. This is my twenty-second year as a professor, and my tenth at the University of South Carolina Aiken."

Hunter raised his hand.

"Yes, Mr. Waters?" Professor Jenkins asked.

"Where did you teach before your time here?" Hunter asked.

The girl to Isabella's right glared at Hunter and moaned. "Shut up. Nobody likes a teacher's pet," she grunted.

"I taught at Stanford University before moving down south to be closer to my children and their families," Professor Jenkins replied.

"Which school do you like better? I imagine it has to be really different teaching at such a small school like USC Aiken after being at a university like Stanford," Hunter said.

Isabella looked at Hunter with eyebrows raised, unsure of what to think about his sudden interest in their professor.

"I appreciate your questions, Mr. Waters, and would be glad to discuss my teaching background at another time. However, I'm afraid we must focus our time in class on the biological sciences rather than personal history," Professor Jenkins said.

The professor took a swig from his cup and directed his attention back to the class as a whole.

"Now, I know you are all thrilled at the opportunity to attend a Thursday night lab, so let me add to the already pleasurable experience." Professor Jenkins paused before continuing. "Attendance is mandatory. Every absence will result in the loss of a letter grade. Miss more than three labs and you'll fail the class. Plain and simple."

For the first time since she'd sat down beside her, the girl next to Isabella raised her head and looked up at the professor. "You serious?" the girl asked.

Professor Jenkins looked for the face behind the voice. His eyes landed on the girl. "I'm as serious as a heart attack," he said.

"This is nuts. I'm out." The girl grabbed her backpack, stood, and walked toward the door. Before she exited the room, she turned to the class. "Y'all best run while you can. There's easier classes than this one."

Isabella watched the girl leave. She looked at Hunter who had a huge grin spread across his face.

"That girl's got guts," he whispered.

Professor Jenkins took a long drink and adjusted his glasses. He walked out from behind the table and stood beside the empty chair where the girl had previously sat.

"She's right, you know," Professor Jenkins said. "There are easier biology classes at this university. After tonight, some of you may find that you're better suited for those classes. Many of you, however, will stick around either because this class is required for graduation or because you want to prove to yourself that you can handle the course. Regardless of your reasons for staying, I can guarantee that you'll emerge with more knowledge about the workings of the world than you would have imagined."

Professor Jenkins returned to his place behind the table, facing the students. He picked up a piece of chalk and turned to the blackboards that covered the front wall of the classroom. The shuffling of papers and the clicking of zippers echoed through the room as the students located paper and pencils to take notes.

"While I write some basic equations on the board, take a moment to meet your table mates. In the coming weeks and months they will become some of the best friends you'll ever have.

I've seen first-hand the close relationships that form through times of trial," Professor Jenkins said with a wink.

Immediately the room filled with thirty voices as the students introduced themselves to their neighbors. Isabella turned to find Hunter already staring at her.

"Well, you heard the man. Looks like we're going to be best friends. Tell me about yourself, Isabella," Hunter said.

"What would you like to know?" Isabella asked.

"Anything you want to tell me," he replied.

"Let's start with three things about each of us, okay?" Isabella asked.

Hunter nodded. "Sounds great."

"Okay, well one is that I live with my dad and step-mom, but I have a great relationship with my real mom, too. It hasn't always been like that, but when I found Jesus two years ago, I realized that a lot of things in my life needed to change. I started going to this awesome church and met some really great people who challenge me in my faith and encourage me to keep walking with God." Isabella paused. "I think that might be two and three?"

Hunter's brow was wrinkled in thought. "Yeah, I think that was enough. So you're a church girl, huh?"

"I've never really thought of myself as 'church girl.' Actually, I'm not like most of the girls I know at church. They've all grown up in the church. They always have the perfect answers to my questions and never seem to have questions themselves. I'm still learning, but I'm loving life more now than I have in a very long time," Isabella said. "But enough about me. Tell me about you."

Hunter hesitated. "I'm not really that interesting," he said.

Isabella punched him in the arm playfully. "Oh, please. Don't give me that. You just practically assaulted the professor before he even stepped in the classroom. I have no doubt you live a crazy-awesome life."

Hunter smiled. "I guess it's not so dull all the time. Let's see. I was born in Washington but grew up in North Carolina. I came to USC Aiken because it is close enough to home that I can get back for an emergency, but it's far enough away that I can have my own life. I also have a secret love affair with Mexican food." Hunter paused and rested his head in his hands.

"That's two," Isabella said laughing. "I know you can come up with one more."

Professor Jenkins stopped writing and grabbed his drink as he stepped away from the board. "Class, let's quiet down. I would suggest you copy these formulas into your notes, but of course I can't make you do anything. We'll discuss them together and work a few problems before you begin your first lab assignment."

Isabella turned back around in her desk and copied the equations into her notebook. She had finished writing the first one when she felt a pencil eraser jab her upper arm. Hunter was staring at her. She raised her eyebrows in question.

"Three. I've never really believed in your whole God thing because I don't see how He could love someone like me. According to a lot of my old friends, God likes people who don't make mistakes," he said. A sad smile curved his lips. "But I'm glad it works for you."

Without another word, Hunter opened his notebook and copied the professor's notes, leaving Isabella to sit in silence and wonder what her new friend could have done that would make him believe that he was unlovable.

*

Isabella parked her car behind the four other vehicles that lined the street in front of her Bible study leader's house. She grabbed her Bible and notebook from the passenger's seat and jogged up the sidewalk to the front door. Her knock was met by a "come in" from somewhere inside the house.

Isabella pushed the door open and stepped into the hallway. Her leader, Tracy Fields, emerged from the kitchen, her arms outstretched for a hug.

"Oh, Isabella, it's so good to see you!" Tracy said.

Isabella bent down to hug her leader. Tracy Fields was five feet tall when she stood on her tiptoes. In her early sixties, she was the mother of two grown children and had a grandchild on the way. She had been happily married for forty years and was active at church. Not only did she lead Bible study for a group of college girls on Monday nights, but she also taught twelfth grade Sunday school at church on Sundays and she and her husband led the same group of young girls and guys in a co-ed study on Wednesday nights. Her once blonde hair was now streaked with grays and whites and she talked faster than a second grader the day after Halloween.

"Hi, Mrs. Tracy. It's good to see you, too," Isabella said. "I'm so sorry I'm running late again. I hate that y'all always have to wait on me."

"You're fine, honey," Tracy said as she pushed the front door closed. "The other girls are in the kitchen eating, so you haven't missed a thing."

Tracy wrapped her arm around Isabella's waist and guided her through the living room to the kitchen where the other girls stood around an island snacking on fruit, cookies, and crackers.

"Go ahead and get something to eat," Tracy said as she pulled a cup out of the cabinet for Isabella. "What can I get you to drink?"

"Sweet tea would be great," Isabella said as she popped a cheese cube and a cracker in her mouth. As she reached for a carrot, her hand knocked over the bottle of ranch dressing. "Wow, am I glad that was closed," she said with a nervous giggle. "I'm so clumsy sometimes."

Tracy handed the cup to Isabella and grabbed a handful of grapes. She headed toward the stairs on the opposite side of the room. "If you girls are ready, let's head upstairs and get started. I want to be respectful of everyone's time, especially since your classes just started last week."

The girls grabbed the plates of food and their drinks and followed Tracy up the stairs to the den situated over the garage. The small room was crowded with old furniture, which made it appear smaller than it really was. The walls were adorned with paintings passed down from Tracy's parents. In one corner, a computer sat alone on a large wooden desk. Another corner housed the television the group used to watch their Bible study lesson each week.

Isabella set the plate of food she carried on a small side table with a glass top and settled into her favorite spot on the floor by the window. Several of the girls plopped down on the couch that faced the television. One of the girls, Dani, set her drink down and looked at Isabella.

"Are you sure you don't want to sit up here?" Dani asked.

Isabella shook her head. "No, I'm good."

"Then here. At least take this to sit on. It has to be more comfortable then the floor," Dani said as she tossed Isabella a pillow from the couch.

Isabella didn't know Dani that well. Dani was the oldest of the girls in the group and was also the only one to have been homeschooled through high school, so their paths had never really crossed. A member of the college cross-country team, Dani was tall and athletic. She was soft-spoken and rarely talked, but when she did, her words were always kind and encouraging.

"Thanks," Isabella said as she slipped the cushion beneath her. She grabbed a blanket from the pile stacked beside the television stand and wrapped it around her shoulders.

"Everybody okay?" Tracy asked as she pulled an old wooden chair over to join the circle the girls had formed around the television.

"Yes, ma'am," Dani replied.

"Great. I thought we'd do something a little different tonight and start with prayer requests. We've been running a little long lately. I understand if you need to leave before we're done, but I'd rather you miss the last few minutes of the video than the opportunity to share the ways we can be praying for each other throughout the week. Is that okay with everybody?" Tracy asked.

All of the girls nodded.

"Great. Okay, who would like to start?" Tracy asked.

Dani raised her hand first. "For me to find the balance between school and cross-country. Both take a lot of time, and since I've never run long distance before, I'm really having to work to keep up with the other girls on the team. We started practicing a month before classes started and our first meet is in a few weeks, so I'm just hoping that that goes well."

Tracy nodded as she added Dani's request to her prayer list. "Got it. I can't imagine trying a new sport for the first time in college. We'll definitely be praying for that."

"Thanks," Dani said.

Isabella raised her hand slowly.

"Go ahead, Isabella," Tracy said.

"I have two, actually. Is that okay?" she asked.

"Of course," Tracy said. "What've you got?"

"I feel kind of ashamed to say this at Bible study," Isabella looked at the faces around her before she continued, "but it's been bothering me. Over the summer, I felt like God told me that He wanted me to spend more time in his Word and to mark the passages I read each day with sticky notes." She held out her Bible so that the group could see the pink, yellow, blue, green, and orange sticky notes sticking out of the book from all angles. "The past few weeks I've made it a priority to read my Bible and pray daily, but I haven't really felt God's presence. When I pick up my Bible, it seems like I'm turning to the same passages I've read before and that I'm not getting anything new out of it. Don't get me wrong, I know the verses are good and all, but they're the ones I first read when I was saved. The ones about how everyone is a sinner, that the punishment for sin is death, and that all people can be saved if they'll just admit their sin and ask Jesus to forgive them. I know those things now. I guess I kind of thought God would want to tell me something new by this point in my life."

Tracy spoke up. "I've been right where you are, Isabella, and it's not easy. Let me share something with you that a friend shared with me during that time. I don't remember the exact text, but I do know it was written by John Piper. He's a respected Bible scholar. He posed the question: why is it that absence makes the heart grow fonder while familiarity breeds contempt? And he answered it by saying that deprivation, or the absence of something, makes desire stronger. It was a hard lesson to learn, but I found that after the dry season where I couldn't hear God, I found him with an even greater passion than ever before," Tracy said.

"Wow, I've never thought of it like that," Dani said.

"Me, neither," echoed Isabella. "Thanks, Mrs. Tracy."

"You're welcome, honey. The Christian life isn't always an easy one, but it's certainly worthwhile," Tracy said.

"That reminds me of my other prayer request," Isabella said.

"Go ahead," Tracy prodded as she finished the note she was making in her journal.

"There's this guy that sits beside me in my biology lab. His name is Hunter. When we met last Thursday night, he was really friendly until I mentioned that I was a Christian. After that he got kind of quiet and told me that God wasn't for him because he had done too many bad things. He didn't give me details, but he said that his friends had told him God couldn't love him because of his past," Isabella said. "I'd just really appreciate it if you guys would pray for him, and I guess for me, too. I want to share Jesus with him, but I want to wait until the right moment."

"Wow, that's a hard one," Dani said. "But I remember having those same thoughts – that God and His forgiveness were too good to be true. It took a while and a lot of searching the Scriptures, but the forgiveness I found was so refreshing. I'll definitely be praying for Hunter."

The other girls nodded in agreement.

An hour later when the Bible study video ended and the girls said goodbye to each other and Tracy, Isabella's mind wandered to Hunter as she prayed that one day before the semester was over, she would have the opportunity to share Jesus with him.

*

Two months later, Isabella entered the classroom to find Hunter bent over a notebook studying.

"Hey, Hunter," she said. "How're you?"

Hunter looked up from his notebook. "I'm okay, I guess. You ready for this test?" he asked.

"Even if I studied around the clock for a week, I don't think I'd be ready," Isabella said as she sat down in the chair beside him.

Hunter laughed and wiped away the beads of perspiration that had formed along his hairline. "Me, neither. I slept with my book under my pillow last night just in case that whole superstition about knowledge seeping through your pillow into your brain is true," he said.

"You are too much," Isabella replied as she pulled her lab notes and textbook out of her backpack. Her Bible was caught between the books and fell onto the floor beneath the table.

"I've got it," Hunter said. He reached down and picked up the book, dusting off the brown leather cover with his hand.

"Isn't letting your Bible touch the ground a sin or something?" Hunter asked.

Isabella couldn't tell if he was joking or not. She decided to pretend that he wasn't. "Not that I know of. Christians do try to treat the Bible with respect because we believe it's the Word of God, but Christianity isn't just about following a bunch of rules. Besides, I told you I'm not perfect. Remember?" She held out her hand for the book. The colored sticky notes stuck out at odd angles.

Isabella realized she had never gotten around to moving the little slips of paper after her talk with Tracy at Bible study.

Hunter hesitated, the book held tightly in his hands. "So tell me. What's so great about this book anyway?"

Isabella tried to hide the shock she felt. "You've never read the Bible?" she asked incredulously.

Hunter shook his head. "No. But someone read it to me once."

"Oh. And you didn't like it?" Isabella asked.

"Let me ask you a question," Hunter said. "Why do *you* read the Bible? Doesn't it just make you feel bad about yourself?"

Isabella considered his questions before speaking. "I guess sometimes it does, yes. But conviction can be a good thing. I mean, I know I'm a sinner, but the Bible gives me hope. It tells me that Jesus's blood covers all my sins."

"All sins? That's not what I heard. I just can't believe that," Hunter said. "Not after what my best friend told me three years ago. This grace isn't for someone like me."

Isabella placed her hand gently on Hunter's arm. "I don't know what your friend said or what you've done, and I don't need to. But I do know this. God's grace is for everyone and covers everything. There's nothing you could have done in the past or could do in the future that would change the way God looks at you."

Hunter set the Bible on the desk and exhaled deeply. "Isabella, I'm gay."

Isabella looked at him without blinking. "Okay, so?"

"So? Doesn't that change everything? Doesn't the Bible say that gay people go to hell? Don't you want to go sit by someone else for the rest of the semester?" Hunter asked, clearly taken aback by her composure.

Isabella responded slowly. "Well, the Bible does make it clear that marriage is a sacred bond between a man and a woman."

"See?" Hunter said. "That's not me."

"But," Isabella interjected, "it also says that God's grace covers all sin if we ask for his forgiveness. I'm pretty sure you can't do anything that falls outside of the word 'all'."

"It just seems too good to be true," Hunter said. "All my life I've been told that God is mean and unfair and has all these rules He wants you to follow. I don't want any part of a god like that."

"Maybe you should check it out for yourself," Isabella suggested.

Professor Jenkins appeared in the doorway and paused a moment before entering the room, his signature Big Gulp cup in his hand. "Good evening, class. Since Fall Break starts in the morning, my present to you is that you may leave class tonight after you complete your test. We will not continue with new material," he said.

Hushed cheers went up around the room as the students scrambled to put their notes away.

When Isabella bent down to put her notebook in her backpack, Hunter whispered, "Maybe you're right. I don't have a Bible, but I'll think about going to get one and seeing for myself."

Over the next hour and a half, Isabella struggled to focus on the test. Her mind kept wandering to the conversation with Hunter and his last words: *I don't have a Bible, but I'll think about going to get one and seeing for myself.* By the time she reached the final page of the test, she knew what she had to do.

Isabella put the finishing touches on her test and placed her pencil in the front pocket of her backpack. Before she left the table, she slipped her Bible into Hunter's backpack.

"What're you doing?" Hunter whispered.

"I want you to have it," Isabella said. "Promise you'll give it a chance?"

Hunter fingered the cracked spine of the book. "I've never read it before. Where do I start?" he asked.

Isabella smiled as she stood and took her test in her hand. "Start with the sticky notes."

A Key and the Cross

Isaiah 65:24 – Before they call I will answer; while they are still speaking I will hear.

Reese heard the A-C-S chant from the fans and knew that her mom would be standing amid the blue and white crowd pulling for an Alcross Charter School win. With each repetition of the school's name, she allowed herself to absorb the energy growing inside the gymnasium. She took a deep breath and glanced around the court. She noted that each of her teammates was matched up with a girl on Weberton's team. *So far so good*, she thought.

Crouching into a proper defensive stance, Reese bent her knees and held her hands out at her shoulders ready to deflect a pass or shot. Sweat dripped from her brow, but she let it cascade down her face, afraid that any lapse in her focus would give Peyton, the point guard for the other team, the break she needed to beat Reese to the basket.

Peyton Grace Wilkinson was an athlete, and basketball was her sport. Despite only standing five foot four inches tall, she could play with the best of them. Never hesitating to jump into a guys' game of four-on-four, Peyton could dribble circles around anyone – even with her eyes closed – and shoot three-pointers from behind the arc with an accuracy that other players only dreamed of.

She had the ball with only eight seconds left in the fourth quarter of the basketball game, and it was Reese's job to make sure she didn't sink the ball through the hoop before time expired.

The entire game had been a defensive battle. Reese wasn't willing to concede the victory, and her opponent's tenacity suggested that Peyton wasn't either. Since their teams' first meeting two months before, which after four quarters of back-and-forth play had resulted in a come-from-behind Weberton victory on Weberton's home court in the final seconds of the game, Reese had dreamed about this rematch and envisioned the win for her team.

This time around, the Patriots traveled to Alcross Charter's home court, a gymnasium that was actually home to a collegiate team in the area. Unlike at the last meeting, Weberton maintained the lead for much of this game, though Reese's last fast-break layup put her team ahead by two points. She was not surprised that the play Weberton's coach called from the sidelines put the basketball in Peyton's hands. Their small team consisted of six players to start with, and after one player had fouled out in the third quarter, they'd been playing with subs. Weberton didn't have a deep bench, so the girls on the court were not as skilled as the first string athletes. Even with a full, healthy team on the bench, Peyton was by far the best player on the Weberton team and probably the most athletic girl on the court.

    Peyton faked a step to her left, but Reese maintained her defensive stance, which meant Peyton would have to drive to the basket instead of shooting the game winning three-pointer the play was designed to create. As Peyton's feet left the court for a layup, Reese stayed close enough to her body to get a hand in her face without risking a foul and the potential for a three-point play. The ball kissed the corner of the square in the center of the backboard and fell through the net.

    Reese sighed. They were going to overtime.

    The five-minute overtime passed in a blur. Reese's teammates secured several steals early in the period, which they passed up the court to her. She finished the fast break with a layup each time. In just a few minutes, the Alcross Charter squad managed to extend the lead to ten points and maintained it for the rest of the game.

Exhausted and sweaty, but happy, Reese fell into line with her teammates to shake hands with the Weberton girls following the final buzzer. As she passed in front of the scorer's table and with the slap of high fives and "good game" congratulations in the background, Reese exchanged a quick hug with Peyton.

"You played a great game," Reese said, shouting to be heard amid the clapping and shouting of the crowd behind her. "I've got a lot of respect for you."

Peyton patted Reese on the back. "Thanks," she said, grinning. "If we had to lose to someone, I'd hope it was y'all."

Reese nodded and continued down the line, shaking hands with her opponents and teammates. After she had congratulated everyone on the court, Reese walked over to the referees.

"Thanks for calling the game," she said as she extended her hand to each of the three men.

Surprise flashed across their faces. "Sure thing, young lady. You played a great game. Your team is getting better. Keep those girls together, you hear?" the oldest referee said. He was tall, and his black hair was sprinkled with white and gray. He called most of their games and had witnessed Reese's team notch some impressive wins and experience some heartbreaking losses over the first half of the season.

Reese smiled. "Yes, sir," she said and ran off to join her team as they entered the locker room.

*

After the post-game talk in the locker room, Reese and her teammates purchased a variety of candy bars, hamburgers, and Gatorade at the concession stand before scoping out a spot on the bleachers among the fans already cheering on the guys' basketball team.

As she walked toward the blue risers with an orange Gatorade in one hand and a bag of peanut M&Ms in the other, Reese heard a voice behind her.

"Hey, Number Three, good game tonight."

Reese turned to see Peyton standing against the tan concrete wall watching the guys' game. Her long brown hair was pulled up into a bun on the top of her head and held out of her face by an elastic Nike headband. She had changed out of her basketball jersey and into a white t-shirt, black athletic pants, and Nike sandals that were the current fad among athletes.

"Thanks," Reese said, hanging back from the cluster of her teammates as they walked, laughing and joking, toward the bleachers. "You played a great game, too. It was really fun."

"It was. I thought we had you guys for a while there, but I guess it helps to have a deep bench for overtime games. Our girls were so tired. We just had nothing left," Peyton said.

"You're right. It definitely does help to have fresh legs for longer games, but personally, I like smaller teams better. It means more playing time," Reese said with a grin.

"Yeah, I get that for sure," Peyton said. "Who do y'all play next?"

Reese thought for a moment. "I think we travel to Tucker at the beginning of next week," she replied. "That'll be a tough game."

"We played them last week," Peyton said. "You guys can hang with them, but you'll have to play the whole game. Don't give up halfway through."

"Thanks, we'll do our best," Reese said. She looked over her shoulder and spotted her mom waving from the top row of the bleachers.

"I think I'm going to go find my mom so we can cheer on my brother together," Reese said.

Peyton reached out and stopped Reese mid-turn. "Do you think we could trade email addresses or phone numbers? I'd really like to keep in touch since we have so much in common with basketball and all. That way we could tell each other about our games through the rest of the season?"

Reese considered her request for a moment before agreeing. "Sure, we could do that. I'm not much of a phone person, but I do like to email and use Facebook."

"Okay, great," Peyton said. "How about you go ahead and give me your phone number, then I'll call or text you so that you have mine, okay?"

"Yeah, sounds good." Reese rattled off the string of numbers and turned to leave. "It was good to talk to you, Peyton. You really did play great. I'm looking forward to the day when I can watch you play in the big leagues."

Peyton laughed. "I'd love for that to happen, but I'm pretty sure it never will. But thanks. You played great, too. I'll text you my email address soon."

*

Two years later, Peyton leaned into a heavy oak door and stepped into the women's locker room. She waited for her eyes to adjust to the darkness of the empty room, and when they didn't, she groped along the wall for the light switch. Light flooded the room, illuminating the rows of metal lockers neatly stacked with white practice jerseys, multi-colored shoes, and orange basketballs. A dry erase board hung on one wall, the notes from yesterday's film session still visible.

Peyton walked across the room and stood in front of the burgundy locker she shared with another girl on the team. Peyton was not a scholarship athlete at the NCAA Division II college, but after training with the team all summer and surviving the first cut of athletes earlier in the month, she thought she had secured a spot on the team. When the head coach had shown her the locker with her name and number on it, Wilkinson 14, she was surprised to see another girl's name, Moore 21, as well. Although no one had said as much, Peyton concluded that the two girls were vying for the final position on the team.

Since that day two weeks ago, Peyton had put in more hours at the gym than ever before. She ran sprints, lifted weights, and shot free throws in addition to the two a day official practices run by her head coach, Grant Meyer, and his assistant, Pamela Walker. Peyton noticed that not only was she stronger now but also that her shooting percentage had improved. She was convinced that if she had noticed these differences, her coaches must have as well. Surely they were pleased with her progress and saw the same promising future for her basketball career as the one she envisioned for herself.

That was why, when her coach texted her early that morning and asked her to stop by his office before practice, she had smiled expectantly. *I just know he's going to give the twelfth spot to me*, she thought as she stuffed a chewy breakfast bar in her mouth and gathered her basketball gear for practice. But as she drove across town to the college, other thoughts crept into her head, warring for space.

Those were the thoughts that had driven her to the locker room. She needed to quiet the negative voices in her head, the ones telling her that she wasn't good enough, before meeting with her coach.

Peyton ran her fingers across her nameplate, the sharp edges of the grooved letters pricking her skin. She checked her teeth for leftover bits of granola and retied her long brown hair into a bun with a black hair elastic. Satisfied with her appearance, she took a deep breath and crossed the room to the door, turned the light off, and stepped out into the hallway without looking back.

Peyton walked down the long winding hallway toward her coach's office, which was tucked into the back corner of the athletic facility. Her footsteps echoed off the linoleum floor, scuffed from the cleats and tennis shoes that roamed the passage daily. The harsh fluorescent lights reflected off the concrete block walls, causing Peyton to squint against the glare.

She pushed open the glass door to the athletic offices and waited while her eyes adjusted to the dimly lit room. The receptionist's desk was empty since the building wouldn't open to the public for another two hours. Peyton watched the door swing shut behind her, the bottom swooshing against the green carpet as it closed.

Peyton walked across the lobby, weaving between several wooden chairs and a gray leather couch wrinkled from age and use. She rounded several corners and stopped a few feet away from her coach's office.

The door to Coach Meyer's office was cracked. Though Peyton could not see him through the small slit, the clicking of a keyboard and the muffled squeaks of shoes on a court told her he was there. *He must be watching film from last week's scrimmage*, Peyton thought.

She took a deep breath and knocked on the door.

"Come in," a deep voice said from inside the room.

Peyton pushed the door open and stepped into the familiar room. One wall of the room was made entirely of windows that looked out to the parking lot. Pictures of Coach Meyer's family framed the computer that sat in the middle of his immaculate wooden desk. In one corner, a television sat atop a rolling cart. Shelves lined with old film reels and playbooks lined one of the walls, while team posters and old jerseys hung on another.

Coach Meyer, a bald man with a clean-shaven face, leaned forward in the chair behind his desk and clicked off the television. He placed the remote on his desk and motioned for Peyton to sit down in one of the cushioned chairs opposite his desk.

"Good morning, Peyton," Coach Meyer said. "Thanks for coming in early this morning."

Peyton sat down on the edge of the chair. When she noticed that her legs were bouncing erratically and that her knuckles were white from gripping the armrests, she forced herself to relax.

"No problem," she said.

"I want to wait for Coach Walker to arrive before we get started. She should be here in just a moment," Coach Meyer said as he pulled a bottled water out of the mini-fridge hidden behind his desk. "Can I get you anything to drink?"

"No, sir. I'm fine. Thank you," Peyton said. She folded her hands in her lap and leaned back.

If Coach Walker is going to be here, too, this is either going to be really good or really bad, she thought.

"Hey, y'all." A high-pitched female voice floated into the room from the hallway. Coach Walker looked at her watch. "Am I late?"

Peyton glanced over her shoulder and smiled as the assistant coach entered the room and sat in the chair beside her. Coach Walker was tall and thin, with straight bleach-blond hair that stopped at her jawline.

Coach Meyer shook his head. "Morning, Pam. You're right on time."

"Good, good." Coach Walker brushed her hand on Peyton's shoulder. "How are you today?"

"I'm okay," Peyton said. "Thanks for asking."

An uncomfortable silence settled over the room. Peyton held her breath and looked expectantly from one coach to the other. Coach Meyer drummed his fingers on the table. Suddenly, he sat forward in his chair and rested his elbows on his knees.

Drawing a deep breath, he said, "Peyton, I've always been up front with you as a coach, no?"

She swallowed, nodding.

"So I'm going to shoot straight with you now," he continued. "Both Coach Walker and I have been impressed with the effort you've put into your workouts these few months." He looked to his assistant. "We've noticed your improvement, and we're proud of your hard work."

Coach Walker nodded in agreement.

"I want you to know this is a tough conversation to have and that we're not making a rash decision. We've discussed our options and have reached a conclusion." He took a breath and looked directly at Peyton.

She forced herself to meet his gaze, refusing to turn away.

"We want to thank you for your dedication to the team, but we're afraid the road as an athlete ends here," Coach Meyer said.

Peyton stared straight ahead, unable to believe what she was hearing. *This can't be happening, can it? Basketball has been my life since, well, practically forever. I've worked so hard. He said they've noticed.* She felt a hand on her shoulder.

"Are you okay? I know this is hard to hear," Coach Walker said, her brow creased in concern.

Peyton nodded, not daring to look at either of her coaches. "Is that all?" she asked as she stood to leave.

"Not quite," Coach Walker said, rising as well.

Peyton looked at her, her eyebrows arched in confusion. "Okay?"

"We'd like for you to be team manager. You'd still help at practice and travel to all the games with the team. We love your passion and want your positive energy around the girls," Coach Walker said.

Peyton looked at the floor. "Do you need an answer now?" she asked, fighting back the tears that threatened to fall.

"We don't. Take a few days to think about it, and let us know," Coach Meyer said. He stood and moved toward the door. "Thank you for your dedication to the team, Peyton. It hasn't gone unnoticed. We hope you'll decide to stay on with us."

Peyton kept her head down and nodded almost imperceptibly. She walked to the door and slipped into the hallway as the first tear slipped down her cheek.

*

Reese could not have been more excited to be attending the Passion conference in Atlanta, Georgia, with her best friend. The girls had chosen to attend the same college, though they had made their decisions independently, and had grown closer in the days since their first meeting on the high school basketball court. After Peyton was cut from the college team three months ago, her demeanor had changed. She was lost, insecure, and unmotivated. Worried by the change in her friend, Reese invited her to spend a weekend away from school, hoping the conference would remind Peyton of the girl she used to be.

"Hey, Peyton. Wait up!" Reese called as she ran after her best friend. She wove through the crowd of young adults lining up for the first worship session at the annual Passion conference.

Peyton lifted her hand in the air and waited for her friend to catch up. Reese squeezed between two strangers and wrapped her arms around Peyton in a big hug.

"This is insane! Can you believe how many people are here?" she asked as she pulled her hands inside the sleeves of her sweatshirt. She shivered against the cool night air.

Peyton smiled and rubbed her hands up and down on Reese's arms. "You a little cold?" she asked.

Reese nodded.

"And you're right. I don't remember there being this many people at Passion last year," Peyton said.

The Passion conference was a yearly gathering in early January, taking place in the heart of downtown Atlanta, Georgia. Thousands of eighteen- to twenty-five-year-olds invaded the city during the four-day conference, booking hotel rooms or staying with friends and family during the nights and attending worship services, Bible teachings, daily devotions, and midnight concerts.

Though this was the second time each of the girls had attended the conference, it was the first time they'd come together. The college ministry at Reese's church had reserved several spots at this year's conference, and she had finally cajoled Peyton into coming with her.

The marquee in front of the Staples Center flashed red, and large black numbers appeared on the sign.

Reese squeezed Peyton's arm. "This is it! The countdown!"

Peyton laughed at Reese's childlike excitement. "I've been to Passion before, silly. Remember?"

Reese smiled. "I know, but how are you not just so excited right now!" she exclaimed. "I am so glad you decided to come with me this year." She turned her eyes back to the sign on the outside of the arena and watched the final seconds tick off the countdown. 5... 4... 3... 2... 1.

A roar rose from the crowd, shattering the stillness of the night. The doors to the arena opened, slowly drawing the crowd toward them. Reese latched onto Peyton's arm so that the movement of the crowd would not be able to separate them as they rushed toward the doors.

After what seemed like hours of being carried along by the crowd, the girls found themselves inside the arena. Reese followed Peyton up the stairs to the second level where they found a pair of seats together near the end of an aisle.

Reese leaned over and yelled into Peyton's ear so she could be heard over the buzz of the massive crowd filing into the arena for the opening session of the conference. "These are great seats. Good choice," she said.

Peyton smiled. "They are really good. Want to map out a plan for tomorrow?" she asked.

When Reese nodded, she pulled the weekend's program out of her back pocket and unfolded it across her lap. Reese tilted her head and looked over her friend's shoulder. Her eyes scanned the paper as she read about each of the activities scheduled to fill the next three days.

"What do you want to do?" Peyton asked.

"I want to do it all," Reese replied.

Peyton rolled her eyes. "No surprise there, my friend. We'll try to do it all for sure, but what's like, something you definitely don't want to miss?" she asked.

Reese looked across the arena as her mind ran over the list of possibilities. The arena was already over half-full and a constant stream of people continued piling in from all directions. The noise was growing to a dull roar and the lights of cell phones dotted the darkness, making the floor resemble a clear night sky.

"I think I want to do Kneel," Reese said after a long pause.

Peyton tilted her head in confusion. "Kneel? What's that?" she asked.

Reese reached over and took the program from Peyton. She flipped it over and pointed to the section that talked about Kneel. Peyton's eyes scanned the program.

"You want to do the prayer thing?" she asked when she finished reading the description.

Reese nodded. "I do. It's like a guided prayer experience. There are ten stations that have prayer prompts, like suggesting things for you to pray for." Reese paused to make sure Peyton was listening. "And it ends in the Cross room. I didn't do it last year, but one of the girls from my church did and said it was amazing."

When Peyton raised her eyebrows, Reese sensed her hesitancy. "We don't have to do it if you don't want to," she said.

Peyton shook her head. "No, I want to. I'm just not the best pray-er. You know that."

Reese smiled. "I know, but you don't have to pray out loud, you know? Like, it's just a silent thing, I think."

"Yeah, you're right," Peyton said. "Okay, let's do it."

"Yes! We can go by and pick out a time after worship tonight," Reese said. "I read that you have to reserve a time slot so that it doesn't get too crowded at any one time."

*

"Okay, so was that awesome or what?" Reese asked, practically bouncing with excitement as she followed Peyton out of the morning session the following day.

"It *was* pretty good," Peyton agreed, a small smile playing on her lips.

"Come on. It was better than good, and you know it," Reese said.

When Peyton only nodded, Reese stopped and pulled her friend aside. "Hey, what's wrong? Like, really?"

"Nothing's wrong. I'm good," Peyton said.

Reese rolled her eyes and led her to an empty bench on the outskirts of the commotion in the room. "You forget that I know you way better than that," she said. "We talk, remember?"

Peyton sighed and bit the corner of her lip. "I think maybe I just kind of felt like John Piper was talking directly to me, you know?"

Reese crossed her arms. "I'm not sure I understand," she said.

"I guess that after everything that's happened with the basketball team and being demoted to manager and all, I felt like his message was just for me. Like, be content where you are, find your identity in who Christ says you are instead of what men declare you to be... all of it really," Peyton said, her eyes growing misty.

Reese nodded. "I totally get that," she said slowly. "I know it's really hard for you to be around the team all the time and not like 'be' on the team, especially when you love the game so much, but in case I haven't told you, I'm really proud of your attitude about it."

"Thanks," Peyton said as she dabbed at the corners of her eyes. "That means a lot, but if I'm telling the truth, my attitude really isn't that great all the time."

"You could've fooled me," Reese said as she stood. "Are you ready to find Kneel?"

"Sure," Peyton said as she followed Reese toward the stairs.

The girls rode the elevator to the top floor. The doors opened, revealing a large lobby that looked much like the conference room on the first floor. The walls were the same shade of off-white and the floors were covered in burgundy carpet.

"Looks familiar, huh?" Peyton said.

Reese nodded. "Exactly the same. Well, except without all the people. It's so quiet up here."

"It is. So where do we go now?" Peyton asked.

"I think the lady said it was around to the right," Reese said. "Let's go that way and see what we find."

She led the way down the carpeted hallway, passing only one couple before stopping at the entrance to Kneel. A tall volunteer with brown hair and freckles smiled and offered his hand to the girls. "Hi, ladies. I'm Brent. Are you here for Kneel?" he asked.

Reese nodded and pulled the paper key out of her pocket. "Yes, sir," she said.

He took her key and the one Peyton handed to him. "Great. Do y'all know what you're doing? Or I can explain it if you'd like?"

Reese looked at Peyton, who shrugged. "A little guidance would be great," she said.

Brent laughed. "No problem. So what you'll do is enter the guided prayer experience through the gap between those two pillars." He motioned to an open walkway framed by two Styrofoam columns on the other side of the room. "From there, you'll weave your way through the maze of prayer, stopping at each of the stations to pray according to the prompts listed."

The girls nodded.

"Don't feel obligated to pray at each of them and please move at your own pace," Brent continued. "The exhibit is for you, and it's our hope that this can be a peaceful time for you to hear from and talk with God."

Reese smiled. "Sounds great."

"One more thing," Brent said. "The final station of Kneel is the Cross room. There isn't a prayer prompt in there because we believe God has something different in store for each person who enters that room. Before you leave, you'll take a real key from the wall as a reminder that you have unlimited access to the Father."

"That's so cool," Peyton said.

"It really is," Reese agreed. "Thanks, Brent."

"No problem. You ladies enjoy your time," he said.

Peyton followed Reese toward the entrance to Kneel, bumping into Reese when she stopped abruptly.

"So how do you want to do this?" Reese asked.

"What do you mean?"

"Well, like, do you want to go through together, or should we like, just meet up at the end?" Reese asked.

Peyton hesitated. "Let's do that," she said.

"Sounds good," Reese agreed. She wrapped her arms around Peyton. "Thanks for doing this with me."

"No problem," Peyton said. "I'll see you soon, okay?"

Half an hour later, Reese stood in front of the stained wooden doors that separated her from the Cross room. Exhausted from constant intercession for topics ranging from unsaved family members to government officials to missionaries overseas, Reese took a deep breath and pulled one of the doors open.

She stepped into the dark room, lit only by small candles that circled a large wooden cross in the center of the room. Like the rest of the building, the floor was covered with burgundy carpet. A few girls sat with their backs against the wall, heads bent and tucked between their drawn knees. A guy knelt beside the cross, using a pen and sheet of paper provided to write a letter. Others lay prostrate on the ground with cushions under their heads for support.

Reese made her way to an empty corner of the room and slid down the wall to the floor. She crossed her legs and rested her elbows on her thighs, letting her head drop into her hands.

Okay God, I'm here. I'm listening. What is it you want me to pray for? Reese asked silently. She waited for a few moments until she felt the prompting of the Holy Spirit, the inaudible whisper of His voice, and then she prayed in earnest for the soul of her best friend.

A while later, Reese opened her eyes and glanced around the room. Even more people had filled the quiet space since she arrived, each completely unaware of the others. Her gaze settled on Peyton, who was sitting motionless in front of the cross, her head bowed.

Reese stood quietly and walked toward the door serving as the exit to Kneel. Several keys dangled from a long hook beside the doorframe. As she reached out and removed a key from the hook, the ones left behind clanked quietly against each other.

"Shh. People are trying to pray, silly," a familiar voice whispered in her ear. Peyton stepped out from behind Reese and took a key from the hook, stilling the remaining keys with her fingers.

Reese stuck her tongue out in jest and pulled Peyton with her through the door and into lobby. The girls found an unoccupied bench on the fourth floor of the building and sat down facing each other.

Reese opened her mouth to speak, but before the words could slip out, Peyton said, "Okay, so guess what?"

"I have no idea?" Reese asked.

A smile spread across Peyton's face. "I rededicated my life."

Reese's mouth dropped open. Hundreds of thoughts raced through her mind, but she couldn't form a coherent sentence.

"Reese, did you hear me?" Peyton asked, her eyes growing misty for the second time that day. She shook, her friend's shoulders gently. "I rededicated my life to Jesus."

Reese couldn't contain her wonder any longer. "Oh my gosh, that's so great!" she exclaimed. "I'm so proud of you! Tell me all about it."

Peyton shrugged. "It happened in the Cross room. It was just so peaceful, and I felt like

Jesus wanted me to give the number one spot in my life back to Him." Once she started speaking, words rushed out in a constant stream that couldn't be stopped. "I think I had kind of put basketball above Him, almost as like an idol, and He wants that place. I think He wants to show me that He is enough for me, that I don't have to be defined by my role on the basketball court. Basketball isn't my identity – at least it shouldn't be. *He* should be where I find my worth."

Reese leaned forward and threw her arms around Peyton, tears of joy dropping onto the girl's gray sweatshirt. "I can't even believe this." She sat back and dried her eyes with the sleeves of her jacket. "God, you are just too good," she said aloud.

Peyton raised an eyebrow in confusion. "God is definitely good and all, but am I missing something?"

Reese laughed through happy tears. "Maybe a little. You'll never believe what God did just now."

Peyton sat silently, waiting for an explanation.

"It was the weirdest thing," Reese began. "When I was in the Cross room, I asked God what He wanted me to pray for, and I had the strongest urge to pray for you. For the past half hour I've prayed unceasingly that God would soften your heart and that you would listen for what He wanted to do in and through you. I've never heard God so clearly as I did in that room," Reese said as she looked past Peyton to the closed double doors of the Cross room.

Peyton let out a long, slow breath. "Wow. You were praying for me? I had no idea," she said, her voice trailing off.

"Well, I pray for you a lot," Reese confided as the girls stood and walked toward the elevator. She laid her arm across Peyton's shoulders. "It just so happened that today I got to see the fruit of my prayers first hand. Only God could turn a basketball opponent into a best friend, send her to the same college as me, and give me the privilege of praying for her while He works behind the scenes to do the exact thing I'm asking."

More than Just a Goal

Ephesians 3:20-21 – Now to Him who is able to do immeasurably more than all we ask or imagine, according to His power that is at work within us, to Him be glory forever and ever! Amen.

"Molly. Molly, honey, wake up."
Molly's eyes fluttered open. Her gaze was foggy, but through the haze she saw the outline of her husband's head against the harsh fluorescent hospital lights behind him. She blinked, squeezing her eyes shut before reopening them, in an attempt to clear the blurry image of her husband's face peering down at her.

When his brown eyes, rimmed by the black frames of his glasses, and balding head came into focus, she felt the muscles in her arms relax.

Molly managed a small smile. She reached her hand up to brush her blond hair away from her face, noting the many tubes and monitors attached to her arm. As she returned her hand to where it had been laying on the bed, it brushed her stomach, which was less than half the size it had been yesterday. Countless questions warred against each other in her mind. She needed answers. Molly tried to speak, but the dryness of her throat caused her voice to come out in raspy coughs.

"Easy, sweetheart. Let's see if this will help," her husband, Mike, said as he reached for a white paper cup sitting on the tray table beside her hospital bed.

Holding the cup in one hand, Mike slipped his other arm behind her back. She felt his muscles contract as he raised her off of her back. Molly tried to sit up, but the effort elicited a sharp pain that tore through her abdomen.

"Ow!" she cried, letting the weight of her body fall back against her husband's arm.

"Are you okay?" Mike asked, worry and concern deepening the lines around his eyes.

Molly clenched her fists and waited for the pain to subside. She studied the face of her husband. The dark circles under his eyes hinted at the sleepless nights that were now the norm. His usually clean-shaven face was covered in a week's worth of stubble, a testament to their current situation in life – the neonatal unit of the small hospital on the outskirts of Albuquerque, New Mexico.

Molly nodded and pointed at the cup in his hand. She braced herself against the pain as she pushed herself up on her elbows, desperate for a sip of water. The liquid couldn't have been cooler than room temperature, but as the water trickled down her throat, Molly couldn't remember ever having a more refreshing drink. She took another sip before pushing the cup away.

"That's all you want, honey?" Mike asked.

Molly nodded. "Yes. That was wonderful." She licked her chapped lips and looked around the room, taking in her surroundings for the first time.

On the wall across from her bed, a white marker board listed the times and dosages of her medications, as well as the names of her doctor and nurse. A small television sat on a wooden shelf in the corner of the room. To her right, closed blinds hung down over a large window, allowing the sun's rays to peek through the slats and reflect off the sterile white- and gray-checkered tile floor. A wooden chair with a burgundy cushion was positioned in the corner by the window.

Molly turned her gaze from the room to her husband's face. She swallowed and cleared her throat before asking the question that had rattled around in her mind since the moment she awoke to her husband's voice.

"Where are the babies?"

The question filled the silence of the room. Molly placed her hand gingerly on her stomach, flattened by the absence of the triplets she had carried for the past twenty-seven weeks. The triplets had been born thirteen weeks prematurely, before Molly even reached the third trimester of pregnancy.

Mike reached for her hand, wrapping his fingers around hers amid the tangle of tubes keeping his wife alive.

"They're okay for now," Mike whispered, leaning in to kiss Molly on the cheek.

Molly searched for the meaning behind her husband's ambiguous answer, but the relief of knowing her children were alive quickly became the center of her attention.

They're okay! But he said 'for now?' What does that mean? Why just now? she wondered.

"I don't understand," she finally said. "Why just no-"

A knock at the door stopped Molly mid-sentence. Dr. Watson stepped through the doorway, a medical chart in one hand. Tall, dark, in his mid-thirties and with an honorable career, Dr. Watson was the type of man any mother would want her daughter to marry. His white coattails flowed behind him as he pulled up a chair next to Mike.

"It's good to see you awake, Molly," Dr. Watson said as he set the chart on the edge of her bed. He leaned forward and rested his elbows on his knees.

Molly smiled and nodded slowly. "Thank you, Doctor." She looked from Dr. Watson to Mike. "Well, where are they?" she asked, her voiced strained with impatience and fear.

Dr. Watson took a deep breath. "The triplets are being cared for. They're just down the hallway," he said as he motioned toward the door.

He said 'triplets.' That must mean they're all okay, Molly reasoned.

"When can I see them?" she asked, turning to her husband for support.

Dr. Watson pursed his lips and leveled his gaze at Molly. "I'll have a nurse bring a wheelchair and take you to them." He paused. "But Molly, they're very small and very sick. You need to understand that."

Molly hesitated. "But they're alive. They're going to be okay," she said. The words were more a question than a statement.

Dr. Watson placed a hand on Molly's foot. She felt the warmth of it through the thin white sheets covering her body. "They're doing as well as can be expected at this point. The oldest, one of the two girls, is in the worst shape. The boy is the smallest. The healthiest only weighs two pounds, two ounces. They're far from out of the woods," he said solemnly.

Molly's breath caught in her throat as she tried to process the information the doctor had just rattled off. Her eyes filled with tears, and before she could stop them, they rolled down her cheeks, releasing the fear, anger, hurt, and anxiety that she'd kept bottled inside for months. She had felt alone during much of her pregnancy, fearing for the lives of her unborn babies, while her husband traveled around the country as his job required. Molly was thankful Mike had a job to provide for their growing family, and she knew the travel was necessary, but in his absence, she'd been forced to endure the various medical tests and receive the troubling news about the health of the babies from her doctors alone.

Mike took her hand, squeezing it gently in his strong grip. "It's going to be okay, honey," he said. "But I need you to fight, to get stronger. The kids are going to need you."

Molly nodded, wiping away the tears with her free hand. "You're right," she agreed. Turning to the doctor she said, "When can I see them?"

*

Molly leaned against the side of the plastic hospital bassinet, her finger wrapped inside the small fist of her son, Layton. She studied his delicate features through the tubes that connected his body to the machines and monitors that whirred in the background, keeping the child alive. His eyes were closed, the paper-like lids hiding his blue eyes from view, and his bottom lip protruded as if he were pouting.

Molly shifted her gaze to the little girl lying alone in a bassinet beside Layton. At birth, Cassidy was both the youngest and the largest of the triplets. In the month and a half since her birth, she had gained a couple pounds and had weighed in at just over four pounds yesterday. During his morning rounds, Dr. Watson mentioned that if Cassidy continued growing at the current rate, she could be released from the hospital in another month. Even with her weight gain, Cassidy looked so small in the double bassinet that she had shared with the other triplet, Shelby, just last week.

As she leaned back into the hard hospital chair, Molly closed her eyes. The past few days had been harder than she had imagined. Nothing could have prepared her for the task of saying goodbye to Shelby, the oldest of the triplets, Sunday morning. The words her mother had whispered in her ear following the death of Molly's younger brother when he was just two years old flooded her mind. "Parents should never have to bury their children," her mother had said.

She had been right, of course. The physical pain and emptiness of the emergency cesarean section was nothing compared to the emotional pain and sense of loss that accompanied Shelby's burial in the small cemetery at the back of the hospital grounds. Molly knew she wasn't supposed to be mad at God, but she also felt like He deserved her anger. She'd asked Him to protect all of the triplets, not just two of them, and yet He had let one of them die.

The click of the door opening behind Molly interrupted her thoughts. She turned to see who had entered, smiling when she recognized her friend, Lynn.

"Hi, Molly," Lynn said as she approached the young mother and the two sleeping infants. In addition to the sterile hospital gown she had been issued, Lynn wore paper medical booties, which kept her shoes from squeaking on the shiny tile floor.

In her early fifties, Lynn was more than a decade older than Molly, with three grown children of her own. The two had met while rocking babies in the nursery at church, and both shared a love for children. Lynn was short and stout, her jet-black hair streaked with gray.

Molly stood and hugged her friend. "Hey, Lynn. Thanks for stopping by," she said as she pulled up a chair beside her for her friend.

"How are you doing today?" Lynn asked, as she took a seat. She placed a hand on Molly's knee.

Molly considered the question. "I'm doing all right," she finally said, deciding that was the most truthful answer.

Lynn nodded and looked at the sleeping children. "They're beautiful," she said.

Molly smiled and nodded. She swallowed past the lump that had formed in her throat. "When the doctor came by this morning, he was pleased with their progress. Layton still has a long way to go, but Dr. Watson said Cassidy may be healthy enough to be discharged in a month or so."

"That's wonderful, dear," Lynn said. The corners of her eyes crinkled when she smiled. "Is Mike off-duty today?"

"Something like that," Molly said. "He's actually back home in Santa Rosa working for the next three days. With the funeral earlier this week, he missed several days in the office," Molly said.

Lynn scooted her chair closer and wrapped her arms around Molly's frail shoulders. "What can I do for you?" she asked as she smoothed Molly's hair with her hand. "Can I bring you food? Sit with the children so you can nap for a few hours? You looked exhausted. How long have you been here?"

Molly smiled at the peppered questions, relishing the safety and control she felt when in Lynn's presence. "We have enough meals in the freezer at the apartment to last us several weeks," she said, glancing down at the silver watch on her wrist. "And I've been here with the kids for about ten hours. I'll stay for another four or so, head to the apartment to sleep for a few hours, and be back in the morning."

"That's fourteen hours, honey," Lynn said, her eyebrows raised in shock. "When was the last time you ate?"

"One of the nurses brought me a sandwich about an hour ago," Molly said. "I appreciate your concern, but I really am doing okay," she added, hoping to reassure the older woman.

Lynn shook her head. "Kids these days," she said with a wink. She stood and pushed her chair back against the wall. "I see there's no persuading you otherwise. I'll leave you alone with the little ones," she said as she glanced at the sleeping forms swaddled in pink and blue fuzzy blankets, "and I'll be back to check on you in the morning. I'll bring breakfast."

Molly smiled. "You don't have to do that, Lynn. I'll be fine. Promise."

"I know I don't have to," Lynn said as she wagged her finger at Molly. "But with Mike out of town, someone's got to make sure you're taking care of yourself."

Molly tried to object, but Lynn held up her hand. "No arguing. I'll see you in the morning."

*

"Shh, it's okay," Molly whispered into her son's ear, trying to soothe him and stop his crying. She readjusted the baby in her arms and leaned back into the threadbare sofa cushion.

Molly looked at the digital clock on the microwave. 6:25. *Mike should be home by now*, she thought. She held Layton close to her chest and kissed the top of his head. Despite her fear and exhaustion, she smiled at the fact that at ten months old, he finally had some down-soft hair.

Layton had been crying nonstop for more than twelve hours, and Molly had tried everything she could think of to get him to stop. He didn't want to nurse or suck on his pacifier. Lying beside his twin, Cassidy, hadn't relaxed him, nor had driving around town in his car seat. It didn't matter if Molly rocked him, walked with him, or sat with him in her lap, because nothing could stop the tears.

Molly grabbed the baby monitor from the wooden table beside the sofa and held it up to her ear. She could barely make out the soft breathing of her daughter asleep in the next room over Layton's whimpers but sighed in relief at the sound of Cassidy's rhythmic breaths. Thankfully, with the exception of her post-breakfast meltdown, the girl had slept much of the day.

Molly heard a key inserted into the back door and turned to see her husband as he pushed it open and stepped inside the living room. Even from a distance, Molly could see the dark circles under his eyes from nights spent awake with the twins.

"Hi, honey," Molly said over Layton's cries.

Mike set his briefcase by the door, hung his coat on the door handle, and joined his wife on the sofa. He leaned over and kissed her on the cheek before wiping at his son's tears with his finger.

"What's wrong with Layton?" he asked.

Molly saw her worry mirrored in her husband's face. "I don't know. He started crying the minute he woke up this morning and hasn't stopped since. I've tried everything. I can't make him stop," she said, tears rolling down her face and mixing with her son's.

Mike put his arm around Molly and pulled her close. "Have you called the doctor? Maybe he'll know what to do."

Molly shook her head. "I thought about it, but we were just in there with the kids last week. He said they were fine. I thought maybe Layton was just having an off day, but now, I'm not so sure."

"I'll give him a call and see what he says, okay?" Mike said as he stood and walked toward the kitchen where the phone hung on the wall. "I'm sure the office is closed for the day, but he gave us his home number, didn't he?"

"Yes. I taped it to the fridge," Molly said. She started to get up from the sofa, but Mike shook his head and motioned for her to stay.

"You sit there with him so that I can hear Dr. Watson clearly," Mike said.

Molly nodded. "Okay, but hurry. I just don't know what to do."

*

Less than two days later, Molly sat beside her husband in a small, bare hospital room. She laid her head on Mike's shoulder and allowed her eyes to close for the first time in two days. Layton had finally stopped crying and lay sleeping beside his sister in a small crib on the other side of the room.

"You okay?" Mike murmured into Molly's ear.

She nodded. "Yes. I didn't know it was possible to be this tired," she said.

Mike chuckled softly. "When everyone warned me that having children would cut down on my sleep, I never imagined it would be quite like this."

Molly feigned surprise. "You mean you didn't expect your ten month old son to cry for fifty-seven hours straight and be airlifted to the hospital in Los Alamos? How could you not have seen that coming?" She shook her head. The events of the past four days were stranger than fiction. If she hadn't lived them, she never would have believed something like this could happen.

"Life has a way of throwing curveballs from time to time," Mike said and kissed his wife on the cheek.

Molly opened her mouth to reply but stopped when she heard footsteps in the hallway outside the door. She turned to see the coattail of the on-call doctor as he talked in hushed tones with someone who was hidden from her view.

"I've been praying for answers. Do you think the doctor will have some for us?" Molly asked.

Mike shrugged. "I'm not sure there are answers. After all, this is the same child that has kidney stones, the only infant in the world with that kind of rare kidney condition."

Molly heard a sharp knock on the door and turned to see Dr. Hargrave approaching, a clipboard in his hands. The doctor was short and round. He was in his late sixties and what little hair he had left on his head was a mixture of silver and white. He wore thick glasses to read, though they sat atop his head more frequently than they were used.

"Good evening, Mike, Molly," Dr. Hargrave said.

"Hi, Doctor," Molly answered. "Can you tell us what's wrong with him?"

Dr. Hargrave walked past the chairs the couple sat in and studied the sleeping infants in the crib. He held the clipboard close to his face and fumbled with his glasses, then shook his head.

"It's the strangest thing," Dr. Hargrave began. "In my over thirty years in this practice, I've never seen anything like this. All of the tests have come back negative, and all of Layton's blood counts are in the normal range."

Molly looked at Mike before asking the question she assumed was on both of their minds. "You're saying there's nothing wrong with him then?"

Dr. Hargrave nodded slowly. "That's exactly what I'm saying." He hesitated then continued. "I saw his tears and heard his cries just as you did, and as a parent myself, I understand that what I'm about to tell you won't be sufficient or answer all of your questions."

When Mike reached for Molly's hand, she took it and held on for dear life.

"I'm sorry. I don't know what was wrong with your son," Dr. Hargrave said. "But, I can tell you that he is okay now and that you and your children can go home in the morning."

*

Four years later, Molly stood outside the babies' bedroom and pressed her ear against the wooden door. She heard soft snores coming from inside the room, turned the brass handle, and pushed the door open. The room was dimly lit by a nightlight that was plugged into an outlet in the corner of the room. The light cast shadows off the twin-sized beds that lined two of the walls and reflected off the wooden floor.

Molly slipped through the opening in the doorway and tiptoed across the room to check on the sleeping four-year-olds. Cassidy was curled up in a ball, her light pink blanket and stuffed bunny wrapped tightly in her arms. Her light brown hair was spread out around her and flowed down below her waist. Molly pulled the top sheet up over her daughter and tucked it around her small body.

Satisfied that Cassidy was warm enough, Molly leaned over Layton's bed and looked down at the older of her two children. He lay on his back with his arms out at his sides and his knees bent. Molly smiled and stifled a laugh as she studied her son's sleeping position. She lifted

Layton's shirt and placed her hand over the hole in his side where the feeding tube had been just days before.

Thank you, Father, for removing the tube. I never wanted him to have it in the first place, she prayed as she rubbed her hand over the soft skin of her son's tummy.

Layton had undergone the gastrostomy four days before his fourth birthday. Despite Molly's objections, Layton's doctors had insisted that the feeding tube was necessary, as he never wanted to eat and was not gaining weight.

The tube had fallen out on its own last week when the kids were playing with some friends at the park. To her relief, Layton's doctor had elected to hold off on reinserting it for a few weeks to see if his appetite would return. Though it had only been a few days since the tube had fallen out, Layton was already starting to eat more.

Molly pulled Layton's shirt back down over his stomach and smoothed his blond hair away from his eyes. She gently grabbed his legs and tried to straighten them, but as soon as she did, Layton unconsciously returned them to their original position. Molly shook her head. Even after the recent surgery where the doctor had cut the tight tendons in the back of his knees, Layton still wasn't growing properly, and he walked with his knees bent at forty-five degree angles. For every answered prayer, every step forward, they seemed to take two steps back. She leaned over and kissed her son on the cheek.

"You keep fighting, my brave little boy," she whispered. "I love you."

*

Parker pulled her dark blue Hyundai Santa Fe into the gravel parking lot across the street from the soccer complex. Cars streamed into the area behind her, and parents pulled small children from the backs of minivans and SUVs in a haste to complete the short trek to the fields before the rec league games started.

After she made her way to the back of the car, Parker opened the hatch and pulled out the tie-dyed blanket she always used as a mat when watching her brother's soccer games. She closed the door of the car and started toward the edge of the gravel lot. The Santa Fe beeped twice when she pushed the lock button on the keyless remote.

Parker used her hand to shade her eyes against the bright rays of the setting sun as she scanned the eight soccer fields situated around the complex's central hub for the green and black jerseys of her brother's fifteen and under soccer team. When she spotted his team's colors on the far side of the complex, Parker jogged across the well-maintained grass fields toward the figures that distance made look like ants.

As she approached the field where her brother would play, she noticed her mom already sitting on the small set of metal bleachers that had been placed beside the white lines of the field's boundaries.

"Hi, Mom," Parker said as she walked over and gave her mom a hug.

"Hi, sweetheart," her mom mumbled around the plastic hair barrette she held between her teeth. "How was the math final?"

"I'm pretty sure I slayed it," Parker said with a wink. "Here, let me help you with that," she said as she grabbed her mom's shoulder length brown hair out of her hands. Parker pulled it back in a short ponytail and secured it with an extra hair tie she had on her wrist. "How's that?" she asked as she leaned over to give her mother a kiss on the cheek.

"That's great," her mom said, removing the barrette from her mouth. "I guess I don't need this after all."

"Hey, Jenny. Can I sit with you guys?" a familiar woman's voice said.

Parker turned to see her mom's friend, Molly, walking toward the bleachers. Molly's short blond hair was curled at the ends, framing her face. Her pale skin and white teeth stood out against her bright pink lipstick.

"Of course you can," Jenny said and scooted over to make room for Molly on the bleachers beside her.

"Are my boys out there?" Molly asked.

Parker squinted across the field. "Isn't that Luke about to shoot?" she asked, pointing to a tall, skinny boy with shaggy brown hair.

Molly looked at where Parker was pointing and nodded. "Yep, that's him."

"I don't see Layton, though," Parker said, her eyes still on the players running around the field.

"I think he's the one sitting on the grass," Molly said. "Why is he sitting down?"

Parker laughed. "Maybe he's tired?" she suggested.

"That boy is never tired, though he deserves to be," Molly said. "Did he tell you he swam his first individual medley – butterfly, breaststroke, backstroke, and freestyle – at the swim meet last night?"

Parker shook her head. "I haven't talked to him yet." She climbed up on the bleachers and sat on the other side of her mother. "Wait! He swam an IM? Isn't that the race where you have to do all four strokes in a row?"

Molly nodded and smiled, her lips pressed together in pride. "It was so amazing!"

"Wow. I'm impressed. I'll have to ask him about it later," Parker said.

"Go ask him now," Molly urged. "He's alone, and there's still half an hour until the game starts. Besides, he's always ready to talk to you."

Parker glanced at the field, and since Layton was still alone, she jogged across the green grass toward him. As Parker approached the teenager, he waved.

"Hey, bud. What're you doing?" Parker asked as she took a seat beside him on the grass.

"Just stretching before the game," Layton said. The grin he was never seen without was plastered across his face.

"I think that's a pretty good idea," Parker said as she leaned back on her hands and crossed her legs in front of her. "You don't want to pull something during the game."

Layton laughed. "Definitely not." He adjusted the black and orange strap on the Rec Specs he wore in place of his glasses during athletic events.

Parker watched as Layton straightened his legs as best he could and reached his arms out to touch his toes. Even as he leaned forward, his knees didn't fully extend. Layton had made huge strides, growing more than a foot over the past few years. He was still incredibly thin and wiry, but he looked much healthier than the twenty-four pounds he had weighed on his seventh birthday when the doctors had labeled him "failure to thrive."

"So I heard you swam your first IM last night. How was it?" Parker asked.

Layton's eyes widened, and a smile spread across his face, revealing the blue and orange rubber bands on his braces. "It was amazing! I got a second wind on the freestyle, and I felt like," he hesitated, "I felt like I could run a marathon!"

Parker couldn't help but laugh at his enthusiasm. "I hate that I missed it. I'm sure you were the one to beat," she said.

Layton raised his eyebrows in amusement. "I'd say I had a solid fifth place finish in my heat," he joked.

"Layton! Come on, buddy! The game's about to start," Layton's coach and father, Mike, yelled from the sideline opposite the bleachers.

"I've gotta go," Layton said as he stood and turned toward where his teammates were gathering by their bench. Suddenly he stopped. "Are you staying for the game?"

Parker nodded. "Sure am. Why?"

"I was wondering if you could tell my mom something?" Layton asked.

"Of course, buddy. What's up?"

Layton cupped his hands around his mouth and spoke just loudly enough for Parker to hear him over the cheering and yelling from the surrounding fields. "Can you tell my mom this is the game that I'm finally going to score a goal in? I can feel it."

*

The referee blew his whistle, calling the athletes from both teams back onto the field. Carson, Jenny's son and Parker's brother, handed the goalie gloves over to one of his teammates before jogging to the line at midfield. Like most of the boys on his team, Carson was tall and thin. His yellow-blond hair was cut short, and his eyes were the purest shade of blue. On the soccer field, he was most easily distinguished from his teammates by the bright orange and yellow cleats he wore.

Molly's eyes drifted from her son's friend to her own son, Layton. He walked up to Carson and held out his hand for a high-five. He stood a foot shorter than just about every other boy on the team, despite being two years older. Although Layton was sixteen, the coaches in the under-fifteen league had agreed that Layton should be allowed to play in the younger age group with his brother so that their father didn't have to split his time between two teams in two different divisions. Carson slapped Layton's hand and held it in a handshake before chest-bumping his friend.

Molly smiled and pointed toward the middle of the field. "Look!" she exclaimed. "Mike's putting him in at forward! Y'all, pray he gets a goal. This momma's been asking the Lord to tilt the world so the ball can go in the net for more than ten years."

The shrill whistle signaled the start of the second half, and for the next twelve minutes, the athletes from both teams chased, passed, and shot the ball at each other's goals without success. Mike called a timeout and motioned for the boys on his team to form a circle around him.

"Why did he do that?" Molly asked as she turned to look at Parker.

"I'm not really sure," Parker said as she leaned back against the row of bleachers behind her. She pulled out her phone and checked it for text messages. "We're up by four goals with three minutes left to play, so I'd guess he's just reminding them to focus on defense. We don't need another goal."

"But we'd take another one," Jenny added with a smile.

Molly nodded in agreement. "Especially from my boy."

Parker smiled and turned to face Molly. "Oh my gosh! I know what Mr. Mike is doing. I can't believe I almost forgot to pass along the message Layton asked me to give you," she exclaimed.

Molly turned her attention to Parker. "Is something the matter? Is he okay?"

Parker nodded quickly and rested her hand on Molly's knee. "Oh, yes. Layton's fine. He just asked me to tell you that this is going to be the game he scores a goal in."

The women turned their attention back to the game as the players took their positions on the field. One of the boys threw the ball in to

Carson from the sideline. He dribbled the ball up the field, weaving his way through several defenders in the process.

"So much for playing defense, huh?" Molly asked as she elbowed Parker in the side.

Parker nodded. "I was definitely wrong. They look determined to score a goal now more than ever. I'm pretty sure this is Layton's chance."

As Carson approached the goal from the right side of the field he juked the final defender with a rainbow kick that sent the ball over his head from behind. He crossed the ball to the center of the field, placing it directly in Layton's path as he ran toward the goal.

Molly watched as the referee placed the whistle in his mouth, his eyes glancing back and forth between his watch and the action that was taking place on the field.

"Shoot, Layton!" Molly yelled from the bleachers.

Layton trapped the ball with his left foot and pushed it forward a few inches. He set his plant foot and drew his leg back before kicking the ball squarely toward the goal. The goalie leaped toward the ball as it soared through the air but fell short as the ball struck the back of the net.

The referee blew his whistle, announcing the end of the game, and the bleachers erupted into cheers. Molly jumped to her feet as tears streamed down her face. She pulled Parker and Jenny up beside her, and the three watched as Layton's teammates rushed toward him. The boys hoisted Layton onto their shoulders and carried him around the field in a lap of celebration before setting him down to shake hands with the other team and congratulating them on a hard fought game.

While the players gathered around their coach for his post-game speech, the women folded the blankets they had used as cushions on the cold, hard bleachers. As they started across the field, Molly placed an arm around Parker and Jenny.

"Can you believe that? This momma is on cloud nine right now," she exclaimed, a wide grin plastered across her face.

"I'm so happy for him. Layton is one of the hardest working, most determined people I've ever met. Plus, didn't you say you've been praying for him to score a goal?" Jenny asked.

Molly nodded, but her words stuck in her throat. Of course she'd been praying for the goal, but she realized she'd been afraid to believe it. After God hadn't answered her big prayer for Shelby sixteen years ago, she had doubted that He would care about something small like a soccer goal.

"That's just like our God. Showing up in the little ways, just because He can. I told you Layton said that tonight was going to be the night he scored his first goal," Parker said, remembering the conversation she'd shared with him just an hour earlier.

"I guess it really shouldn't surprise me," Molly said as the trio continued across the field. "That boy has been defying the odds and amazing the doctors since the day he was born. He wasn't supposed to live or even walk, and sports were out of the question until he begged for the chance to play."

Parker nodded. "I remember you telling me that."

The women stopped several feet away from where the boys huddled in a circle around their coach. Molly pursed her lips and closed her eyes. *God, thank you for being faithful even when I am faithless. That was more than just a goal. It was a miracle for my boy and a gentle reminder of Your goodness for his mother.*

A Different Kind of Healing

John 13:7 – Jesus replied, "You do not realize now what I am doing, but later you will understand."

Jason put his hands on his hips as he bent over and tried to catch his breath. The sweat that had formed on his brow due to the oppressive heat of the late afternoon South Carolina sun trickled down his forehead. It was hot, even for September. He stuck two fingers through the slats of his football helmet's facemask and tried to keep the salty perspiration from hitting his eyes.

At five-feet nine-inches and one hundred eighty pounds, Jason was one of the strongest freshmen on the junior varsity football team. The conditioning and lifting workouts he had completed over the summer had sculpted his body, transforming him from a scrawny middle schooler to a forbidding presence on the high school football field.

"All right. Everyone take your places on the line. We'll run one more play, then break for halftime," the varsity coach, Jed Tucker, yelled through the bullhorn. Coach Tucker was a short man with a close-cropped haircut. He was gruff by nature from the years he had served in the military, and his demeanor was the reason Jason hadn't minded that he didn't make the varsity squad.

Jason glanced toward the sideline where his coach, Brett Harding, called the next play through a series of prearranged hand signals. The JV and varsity football teams shared many of the same plays, but Coach Harding had insisted that his young players learn a few new routes for the intersquad scrimmage. As a right guard, Jason's job remained pretty much the same through every play – block for and protect the quarterback at all costs.

Jason crouched down beside his fellow linemen and placed his fingers on the soft grass. His eyes met the varsity player he would be blocking at his quarterback's command and smiled when he recognized the face of his friend Toby. The boys had met at conditioning over the summer. As a senior defensive tackle on the varsity team, Toby was easily twice Jason's size.

Toby winked, and Jason realized that though they were friends in the weight room, on the football field, he would be shown no mercy.

Jason gulped, and a renewed sense of determination flooded his veins. *This is my chance to show Coach what I can do*, he thought as he gritted his teeth. Jason closed his eyes and listened as the quarterback called out the snap count.

"Down, set. Hut. Hut. Hike!"

At the quarterback's cue, Jason lunged forward at Toby and dug his cleats into the soft grass as he pushed against the defender with all his might. He kept his hands away from Toby's facemask and was careful not to hold the boy's jersey.

Wow! I'm doing this. I'm actually holding Toby back. The thought rushed through Jason's mind as he clenched his teeth and grunted through the pain. He felt his arms getting tired but resolved not to give in to fatigue.

Out of the corner of his eye, Jason saw the quarterback step up into the pocket and survey the field for an open receiver. Just as the boy drew his arm back to pass the ball, one of Jason's teammates stepped on the outside of Jason's left foot, causing him to twist and fall. When his friend, Toby, fell on top of him, Jason felt an intense pain shoot up his leg as everything went quiet. His vision blurred, but even blinking rapidly didn't diminish the fuzzy edges that framed the scene on the field. From his place on the ground, pinned beneath the two-hundred-pound senior, Jason watched as the play seemed to finish in slow motion.

When Coach Tucker blew his whistle, signaling the end of the play and the start of halftime, several teammates ambled over and offered Jason a hand. Through the slats in their football helmets, Jason could see their foreheads wrinkled in concern. Jason tried not to cry out in pain as Toby rolled off of his leg and helped hoist him to his feet.

Jason started toward the near sideline but only made it a few steps before he fell again. Toby rushed to Jason's side and bent over him, his eyes wide in concern. Several JV players joined Toby, their hands on their hips as they waited for instruction on how to help their teammate.

"You okay, man?" Toby asked as he motioned for the guys around him to help Jason to his feet.

Jason nodded and winced as he tried to put weight on his hurt ankle. "I'll be fine." Turning to his teammates, Jason said, "Thanks for helping me up, guys," and limped off the field.

When he reached the sideline, Jason grabbed one of the team's green and orange Gatorade brand water bottles and hobbled to an empty space on one of the aluminum players' benches. He removed his helmet and pushed his damp, shaggy black hair out of his eyes. Jason took a swig of water before setting the bottle on the bench beside him and turning his attention to his injured leg.

Coach Hudson jogged over to Jason and bent down beside the young player. He dropped his clipboard on the grass and placed an arm on Jason's back.

"Are you okay, son? You took a pretty nasty fall out there," Coach Hudson said.

Jason nodded. " I think I'll be okay, but my ankle's really sore," he said as he held his injured foot.

Coach Hudson examined Jason's leg and sighed as he stood. "I don't think it's too serious. Looks like a typical sprain to me, but I do think it'd be best if you sat out the rest of the scrimmage."

"Are you sure, Coach? I think I'm okay. I can walk it off and be ready to play some more. I know I can," Jason said as he pushed himself up off the bench. He gritted his teeth and grunted to keep from yelling out in pain.

Placing a hand on Jason's shoulder, Coach Hudson gently pushed the freshman back down onto the bench. "I appreciate your enthusiasm, son, but I can't let you get back out there like this. Rest up over the weekend. Ice and elevate your ankle, and we'll reevaluate Monday."

"But, Coach," Jason protested, "it's only Wednesday. What about practice tomorrow? And Friday?"

"I'd love for you to come out and watch practice, make sure you know the plays, that sort of thing," Coach Hudson said as he turned toward where the offensive linemen were huddled and waiting for instruction, "but I don't want you in gear or back on the field until next week. You're too valuable of a player and it's too early in the season to risk you injuring that leg worse in practice. Are we clear?"

Jason nodded. "Yes, Coach," he said. He blinked rapidly, trying to keep the tears of anger, pain, and frustration at bay.

"Keep your chin up, son," Coach Hudson said. "It's only for a few days. You'll be good as new in no time."

Jason offered a small smile and tried not to let the dejection he felt play out on his face. "Yes, sir. You can count on that," he said as he watched his teammates take the field for the second half of the scrimmage.

*

By the time Jason's mother, Barbara, picked him up from practice after school the following day, his ankle was swollen and throbbing with pain, but because he didn't want to worry her, he decided to continue hiding the injury.

"How was your day?" his mother asked as she pulled out of the gravel parking lot by the football field and merged onto the road.

Barbara was a short woman with the long dark hair and tanned skin consistent with her Spanish ancestry. She often wore oversized floral dresses and shirts, and today was no exception.

"It was a pretty good day," Jason said, praying she wouldn't see the truth through his lie.

Barbara glanced at him out of the corner of her eye. "You don't look very sweaty for having just come from practice," she commented.

Come on, Jason. Think quickly, you know she's right. Jason looked out the window, careful to avoid his mother's watchful gaze.

"I brought an extra pair of clothes with me today and changed in the locker room after practice," he said. "I'm tired of wearing wet clothes home every day. Plus, they smell pretty bad."

Barbara laughed. "You've got that right, son. I hold my breath every time I put a load of your laundry through the wash," she said.

Jason forced a laugh, willing himself to act normal. He hated lying to his mother, but he couldn't let her know he was hurt. She'd blow everything out of proportion and might not let him play again, even after his leg was better.

As Barbara pulled the gold van into the driveway, she turned to Jason and said, "Go ahead and wash up before dinner. Your father will be home from work in half an hour, and you know he'll be ready to eat."

"Yes, ma'am. I'll be quick," Jason said as he climbed out of the passenger seat. He opened the rolling door on his side of the van and grabbed his backpack and gym bag from the carpeted floorboard.

"Are you coming, son?" his mother called from the doorway that connected the garage to the house.

"Yes, ma'am, just grabbing my things. You can go ahead and finish cooking dinner. I'll close the door and lock up," he said.

"Thank you, Jason," she called, already making her way down the hallway toward the kitchen.

"No, thank you, Mom," Jason mumbled as he slid the van door closed and limped across the cement floor of the garage and into the house.

*

The bell rang, signaling the end of second period. Jason slid out of his desk and slung his backpack over his shoulder as he shuffled toward the front of the room.

"Jason, you're limping. I noticed it yesterday but didn't want to pry. Now I must ask. Are you okay?" his math teacher, Mrs. White, asked from where she stood at the dry erase board.

In her early sixties, Mrs. White had been teaching longer than Jason had been alive. She was tall and thin. Her silver gray hair was cut short around her face. Because of her age, she wore reading glasses, which hung from a beaded cord around her neck when they weren't in use.

"Yes, ma'am, I'm okay. Just a little football injury," Jason said, mustering all the enthusiasm he could manage.

Mrs. White squinted, studying him. *This is what it must feel like to be on trial*, Jason thought. He offered her a thumbs-up and turned toward the door of the classroom and the wave of students filling the hallway just beyond it.

"Have a good weekend, Jason," Mrs. White said as he passed by her desk. "I hope you get to feeling better soon."

"Thank you, ma'am," Jason replied as he continued across the front of the room.

His foot caught on a desk leg, sending him sprawling across the cold vinyl tile floor. Jason covered his face with his hands and cried out as the pain in his ankle doubled in intensity.

"Jason! Are you okay?" Mrs. White screeched as she rushed to his side and knelt beside him.

Jason nodded. He could feel the heat in his face. "I'm okay. I just need to get to class," he said as he got to his feet. He put weight on his foot but cried out as another wave of pain shot up his leg.

Mrs. White frowned and shook her head. "I think you need to wait here with me. I'll radio to the office, and they'll get in touch with your mother. You need to see a doctor."

Jason reached out to grab Mrs. White's arm, but she was already halfway across the room. "Please don't ask them to call my mom," he begged, as the room started to spin and black circles clouded his vision from the pain. "She doesn't know I'm hurt," he whispered as the room faded to black.

*

An hour and a half later, Jason sat beside his mother in an empty orthopedic waiting room. Pictures of muscle groups and bones hung from the walls, and a large, rectangular tank with lots of multi-colored fish sat on a wooden table by the receptionist's desk. He leaned back in the hard wooden chair and straightened his legs. Jason glanced nervously at his mother, who held the manila envelope that contained his x-rays from the radiologist's practice across the street.

"Mom?" Jason asked timidly.

Barbara sighed and turned to him, her face creased with worry. "Yes, son?"

"I'm sorry I didn't tell you about my ankle when it happened last Wednesday. Coach thought it was just a minor injury, and I didn't want to worry you. But I should've been honest and told you anyway. I'm really sorry."

"I know you're sorry, son. And I hope you will tell me next time something happens. Passing out in math class is not normal. Something is wrong," Barbara said as she placed a hand gently on his shoulder. "We just need to figure out what it is so that we can get it fixed."

Jason relaxed under the warmth of her grip. His mother had reacted with more grace and composure than he expected, giving him hope that when the doctors and his coaches cleared him to play, she would agree to let him back on the football field.

"Jason?" A young, blond nurse in light green scrubs appeared in the doorway of the waiting room.

"Yes, ma'am. That's me," Jason said as he pushed himself to his feet.

He limped across the room, his mother trailing behind, and followed the nurse to the first door they came to.

The nurse turned to him and smiled. "The doctor is waiting for you inside."

Jason immediately noticed that the small examination room's white walls were bare except for a single poster of a skeleton.

"You must be Jason. I'm Dr. Barker," the doctor said, holding out his hand.

Jason shook the man's hand and studied the young doctor. Dr. Barker had short black hair that parted on one side. He was taller than Jason by a few inches and wore an unbuttoned white lab coat that stretched below his knees. A black stethoscope hung around his neck.

"Yes, sir. And this is my mother, Barbara," Jason said as he motioned toward his mother.

Dr. Barker shook Barbara's hand as well. "It's very nice to meet you both," he said with a smile.

He's nice. I like him already, Jason decided.

The doctor removed the x-rays from the envelope and slid the first sheet of film into what looked like a small computer screen.

"Are we all set?" Dr. Barker flipped the light switch, clothing the room in darkness, without waiting for a reply.

Jason gasped when he saw the picture of his foot illuminated in the film viewer. The white of his bones contrasted starkly with the black of the film's background. He held his breath as the doctor studied the image, his chin cradled in his right hand.

After what seemed like hours, Dr. Barker turned the light back on. The harsh fluorescent lights reflected off the white- and gray-checkered tile floor, making Jason blink back tears. Dr. Barker crossed the room and stood beside Jason, leaning against the examination table.

"Well, I have good news and bad news," Dr. Barker said.

"The good news first, please," Jason replied. He crossed his fingers, hoping for the best.

"The good news is that it's just a bone bruise. There's no break, fracture, or even chip in the bone," Dr. Barker said.

Jason smiled and hugged the doctor. When he realized what he was doing, he unwrapped his arms from the man and smoothed the front of his white coat.

"Sorry, sir," Jason said sheepishly.

"That's okay, Jason. I'm happy for you, too," Dr. Barker said, laughing.

"What is the bad news?" Barbara asked as she got up from the chair and stood next to her son, laying an arm across his shoulders.

"The bad news is that you'll be out of commission for two weeks. In order to make sure the bruise has time to heal properly, I'm going to put you in a boot. It's just precautionary," Dr. Barker said.

"Only two weeks? That's wonderful!" Barbara squeezed her son's shoulders and leaned in to kiss him on the cheek.

"It is good news," Dr. Barker agreed and turned to Jason. "Let me go grab a boot and I'll show you how to wear it."

Jason nodded and watched as the doctor crossed the room. "Dr. Barker?" he asked.

With his hand on the doorknob, Dr. Barker turned around. "Yes, Jason?"

"Are you sure it has to be two weeks? It can't be any sooner?" He hesitated then continued. "You see, I have a game this week."

*

Two and a half months later, Jason sat with his mother in the same examination room as they waited for Dr. Barker to stop by with the results from the latest tests. Jason's foot was propped up on a stack of pillows as he sat on top of the paper-covered table and leaned his back against the wall for support.

He heard a sharp knock on the door and turned to see Dr. Barker enter the room with a medical chart in his hand. Deep lines creased his forehead as he nodded to Jason and Barbara. Without speaking, he pulled a rolling chair out from under the small desk in the room and sat down in front of Jason and his mom.

Dr. Barker set the chart on the ground, took a deep breath, and looked directly at Jason. "I'll be honest. I don't know what to do at this point. The MRIs and x-rays aren't showing anything out of the ordinary. The fact that you describe the main sensation you're feeling as a burning pain does tell me it's something with the nerves, but I don't know what."

"When we were here a month ago, you mentioned that an extra bone had grown in the back of his foot. Is it still there? Could that be it?" Barbara asked.

"Yes!" Jason interjected. "Remember, I asked you if it would give me superpowers. Unfortunately, you said it wouldn't."

"Ah, yes, the Os Trigonum that grew in your ankle? It's still there, but the swelling around it has gone down, so restricted blood flow is no longer a concern. Surgery isn't necessary," Dr. Barker said.

"Well that's good news at least," Jason said. "Although I still wish it came with special powers."

Dr. Barker chuckled despite the seriousness of the situation.

"So what do we do, Doctor? Surely he isn't expected to live with a stabbing and burning pain for the rest of his life?" Barbara said as she looked from Dr. Barker to Jason.

Dr. Barker sighed. "I've done all that I know how to do. I'll refer you to a pain management doctor. He'll probably put you on several narcotics to help dull the pain, and hopefully after that's under control, he'll be able to wean you back off of them. I'm also going to send you to a neurologist. It concerns me that you can no longer feel when other people touch your foot, but she will be more knowledgeable than me in that realm of medicine. Do you have any questions for me?"

Jason shook his head and looked at his mom.

Barbara's brow furrowed. "So, you're telling me he just has to live with the pain for now?"

Dr. Barker stood and pushed the chair back under the desk. "I'll write him a prescription for some pain medicine today. That should hold him over until the other doctors can work him in. I'll be right back with the script," Dr. Barker said as he left the room.

When they were alone, Barbara hugged her son. Jason laid his head on her shoulder, blinking back the tears that threatened to fall. His mother held him at arms' length and looked into his eyes.

"Are you okay, son? I know that's not the news you wanted to hear," Barbara said.

Jason sniffed and nodded. "It's definitely not, but maybe the new doctors will think of something Dr. Barker missed," he said.

Barbara smiled at her son's optimism. "That's my boy," she said as she reached for Jason's crutches that were leaning against the wall. "Until then, we'll continue counting down the days until you're back on that football field."

*

Dr. Michelle Gardner was one of the county's leading neurologists. Her office was located an hour from Dr. Barker's, and when she heard about Jason's unique case, she had agreed to see him immediately.

Both of Jason's parents had accompanied him to this doctor's appointment, as they were all growing weary in the search for answers. His pain was momentarily forgotten, however, when Dr. Gardner stepped into the room to which he had been assigned.

Dr. Gardner was tall and thin with long blond hair pulled away from her face in a ponytail that trailed down her back. A slightly southern accent colored her words, which, Jason decided, only made her more attractive. Her three-inch heels clicked when she walked, adding a sense of sophistication to her appearance.

"Mr. and Mrs. McGuire?" She smiled as she stuck out her hand to greet Jason's parents.

They nodded and shook hands with the doctor.

Dr. Gardner turned to him. "And you must be Jason."

Jason nodded, though it wasn't really a question. "Yes, ma'am. How are you, Dr. Gardner?"

"I'm doing well. Thank you," she said.

"Do you have answers for me?" Jason asked before the woman even had a chance to sit down.

The corners of Dr. Gardner's mouth turned up, but the smile didn't reach her eyes. "I believe I do," she said.

Jason's heart rate quickened. "Please tell us!" Jason pleaded. "I must know what is wrong with my leg."

Instead of pulling up a chair next to his parents, Dr. Gardner took a seat beside Jason on the examination table. She turned her attention solely on the boy.

"From the moment I heard about your case, I've had suspicions of something called RSD. After I ran you through the battery of tests last week and I received the results, I've tried to find anything else it could possibly be. Unfortunately, I haven't been able to do so," Dr. Gardner said.

Jason cocked his head and asked, "RSD? What is that?"

Dr. Gardner put her hands on the table beside her and leaned back. "RSD stands for Reflex Sympathetic Dystrophy. It's a rare condition that affects the body's sympathetic nervous system. When you fell on your ankle during football, your nerves sent messages to your brain, telling it to feel pain. Basically RSD means that those nerves keep sending the message to the brain, even though your initial ankle injury is healed."

A grin spread across Jason's face. "Okay, so finally I am diagnosed. I have RSD. How do we fix that?"

Dr. Gardner frowned. "There isn't really a fix for RSD, Jason. There are some treatment options like nerve blocks and narcotics, which I will recommend, but those aren't cures. They are designed to help patients cope with the pain."

"But," Jason stuttered. "But I thought that a diagnosis meant I would be one step closer to being healed."

Dr. Gardner placed a hand on Jason's leg. "I know you're disappointed, but I'm going to do everything I can to improve your quality of life. For starters, I'm recommending that you stop wearing the boot. Your ankle isn't broken so it's not doing anything to help. You might try walking with a cane or continue using crutches for a while, but with your level of pain, I'm also going to suggest that you consider using a wheelchair."

"A wheelchair?" Jason cried. "Then everyone will look at me funny. Besides, I'm not disabled. My brain is just confused."

"Of course it will be your decision," Dr. Gardner said. "But I want you to be aware of the possibility." She stood and turned to his parents. "Let me go collect some information about RSD for you to look over. When I return, we can talk about treatment options."

The couple nodded but said nothing. Jason looked at his mother and saw tears trickling down her face. His father, never one to show emotion, sat in the chair, his large hand wrapped around his wife's petite one. Jason noticed his father's lips moving, though no sounds were coming from his mouth. With his head bowed and his eyes closed, Jason knew that his father was praying, something he always did when faced with a crisis. Jason punched his foot and squeezed his leg, hoping to feel something besides the constant pain, but although he saw his hand touching his body, he felt nothing.

*

"Good afternoon, Jason. How are you today?" Mr. Jeffrey asked.

"I'm doing all right," Jason said groggily. He blinked rapidly in an attempt to clear the foggy haze that seemed to fill his head.

In his late twenties, Mr. Jeffrey was almost young enough to be Jason's older brother. He was tall and athletic, with auburn-colored hair cut close to his head. He had a thick, bushy beard that made Jason think a small hamster had taken up residence on the man's face.

Mr. Jeffrey had been Jason's English teacher when he attended classes at Kobalt High School. Because of the pain, Jason and his parents had decided that he would complete his freshman year as a homebound student, and Mr. Jeffrey had been assigned as his mentor. Only two weeks still separated Jason from summer break.

Mr. Jeffrey took a seat in the kitchen chair beside Jason's wheelchair and lifted his worn leather satchel over his head. He set the bag on the floor and pulled out several textbooks, dropping them on the table with a thump.

Jason slid a note across the table.

"What do we have here?" Mr. Jeffrey asked as he examined the piece of paper.

Jason smiled and tried to focus on his teacher, but his vision swam. "It's a note from my doctor saying that I'm legally on drugs."

Mr. Jeffrey raised his eyebrows. "I see. Exactly how many medications are you on?" he asked.

Jason counted on his fingers. "I think eleven altogether. Since I advanced to stage three RSD, which makes my entire leg hypersensitive to pain rather than just my foot, I'm maxed out on the dosages of the seven narcotics, plus the nerve blocks and injections that are supposedly untangling the nerves in my leg. Honestly, I'd like to stop taking all the drugs, though. They make me want to sleep a lot, and the world seems foggy when I take them."

"I'm sorry, Jason. I know it must be frustrating for you, but I'm proud of the way you've handled this whole situation," Mr. Jeffrey said.

"Thank you, sir. I did have a little good news this week," Jason offered.

"What's that?"

"I talked to Coach Hudson and told him I was sorry I wasn't able to rejoin the team this year. He told me to focus on getting better and that he'd save a spot for me on next year's team," Jason said.

"That's great news, Jason," Mr. Jeffrey said. When Jason didn't reply, he continued. "Well, let's get to work, shall we? What subject would you like to start with today?"

"I'm doing okay in English and history, but I need some help with math and science," Jason confessed.

"Okay, then math and science it is," Mr. Jeffrey agreed as he selected the thick textbooks from the stack he had placed on the table.

"Could we start with math?" Jason asked as he pulled his textbook out of the backpack slung over the arm of his wheelchair. He dug around inside the bag for a pencil and piece of paper.

"Sounds good to me," Mr. Jeffrey said. "We're on Lesson 3-6 if I remember correctly."

Jason nodded as he flipped the pages of the book. "Yes, sir. That's the one," he said as he wrote his name in the top right hand corner of the paper and numbered one through twenty down the left margin.

"Oh! I forgot to tell you my other good news. My dad says it's an answer to his prayers," Jason said, turning to face Mr. Jeffrey. "I found out yesterday that I qualified for a two-week experimental RSD trial in Los Angeles! My grandparents are going to stay with my brother and sister so my parents can go with me. We're leaving as soon as the semester ends," Jason said as he turned back to his homework.

*

"How is your pain level today?" the lead doctor of the medical trial asked.

Jason looked at the doctor from his wheelchair, which was positioned in the corner of the testing room. Dr. Bergstrom was in his late seventies. Although his black hair was streaked with the white of old age, his dark skin still reflected his Indian heritage.

Jason considered the question before answering. "On the scale? I'd say it's a seven today."

"A seven," Dr. Bergstrom mumbled under his breath. "That's better than the ten you came to us with a week ago."

Jason nodded rapidly. "Yes, sir. I think the treatments are helping."

"I think they are, too," Dr. Bergstrom agreed. "I see you brought a cane with you today. Is that an elephant head on the handle? Tell me about it."

Jason picked up the cane that was resting against his wheelchair and laid it across his lap, fingering the intricate wooden carving of an elephant head. "It is an elephant. When I first learned I had RSD and might be confined to a wheelchair for the rest of my life, an elderly man at church came up to me and handed me his cane. He said, 'I know you'll use it one day. You need it more than me,' and limped away. I've kept it in my closet ever since, but decided to pack it for the trip out here."

"I see," the doctor said. He cocked his head and studied Jason. "So why did you bring it today? You've been doing treatments twice a day for over a week now, but I haven't seen you come in with anything other than crutches or your wheelchair."

Jason hesitated. "I guess I'm feeling hopeful. My pain is finally starting to decrease, even if it's just for short amounts of time. All I've ever heard from doctors since my injury is that I need to get used to a wheelchair because I'll probably never walk again." He paused and looked Dr. Bergstrom in the eye. "I guess I just want to prove them wrong."

Dr. Bergstrom smiled and made a few notes on the clipboard in his hand. "I can appreciate a young man with heart. Now, which game would you like to play today?"

"I like the spaceship one best," Jason said.

"The spaceship one it is," Dr. Bergstrom agreed.

The doctor set the neurofeedback machine, which was used for the RSD treatments, on the floor beside Jason, and attached the three electrodes to the boy's head. Dr. Bergstrom set the LCD screen on Jason's lap and pushed a series of buttons that activated the machine, which looked like a small vacuum.

"Okay, you're all set. I'll be back to check on you in half an hour," Dr. Bergstrom said.

Jason nodded and turned his attention to the screen as his brain sent information to the machine via the electrodes. The neurofeedback machine was a complicated device, but on the first day of the trial, Dr. Bergstrom had described it to Jason as a mirror for the brain. While Jason directed the spaceship through the tunnels and pathways on the screen, his brain would subconsciously control the speed of the spacecraft as well as the volume of the music and the brightness of the screen. In doing so, his brain was 'fixing,' or reprogramming itself, so that he wouldn't feel the pain in his leg.

When the half hour was up, Dr. Bergstrom returned to the testing room as promised. He removed the electrodes from Jason's head and radioed for the receptionist to send Jason's mother to his room.

"Tell me about your pain now," Dr. Bergstrom said as Barbara entered the testing room.

Jason touched his leg and wiggled it from side to side. "I don't feel any pain at all!" he cried.

Barbara gasped and covered her mouth with her hand.

Dr. Bergstrom's eyes widened. "No pain? Are you sure?"

Jason nodded. "Yes, sir. I'm sure. May I try to walk... with my cane of course?"

"I'm not sure that's wise, Jason. The muscles in your leg are going to be very weak. They haven't been used in more than eight months," Dr. Bergstrom warned.

"Please, Dr. Bergstrom?" Jason begged. "I need to walk out of your office on my own."

Dr. Bergstrom sighed and consented. "Very well." He turned to Barbara. "May I suggest that you walk behind him with the wheelchair. He will tire quickly."

Barbara and Dr. Bergstrom helped Jason stand. He gripped the cane and took a small step, bracing for the pain that might follow. A smile spread across Jason's face and tears blurred his vision when the pain didn't come. He took another step forward and another.

"I can walk!" he cried. "This is the happiest day of my life!"

*

Jason stopped to catch his breath and leaned on the metal handrail attached to the steep staircase at the front of the cathedral. He gripped the head of his cane in one hand and wiped the sweat from his brow with the shirtsleeve covering his other arm.

Jason was five months out from the trial treatment in Los Angeles, and his sophomore year of school was just starting to pick up speed. After the trial, Dr. Bergstrom had found a neurofeedback machine for the McGuires to rent so that Jason could continue the treatments at home. While the treatments had lessened his pain for a time, they were unable to completely reprogram the nerves that connected Jason's leg to his brain. Between the neurofeedback treatments, the nerve blocks, and the biweekly injections that Jason endured, he was able to manage the pain and walk with the aid of a cane, though he had given up on the idea of ever being completely healed.

"Are you sure we have to go to Mass, Mom?" Jason asked his mother as she climbed the steps and looked down on him when she reached the top of the staircase.

"Yes, dear. We are going to Mass. Your father is expecting us," Barbara said.

His mother was soft-spoken, but firm, and Jason knew that what she said was final. He sighed and grimaced as he climbed the rest of the cement stairs. Jason reached the top of the staircase and bent over, gasping for breath. When he straightened and looked at his mother, her brow was creased in concern.

"You are in that much pain?" she asked. "From the injections?"

Jason nodded. "It hurts a lot, Mom. I'm not faking it, I promise."

Barbara cocked her head and bit her lip as her foot tapped the ground. "Your father thinks we are coming to the service," she said finally. "Let's go in and see if the pain leaves when you sit down. If it doesn't, we don't have to stay, and I'll take you home, okay?"

"Yes, ma'am. I will try," Jason agreed as he followed his mother to the door of the cathedral.

Barbara held the heavy wooden door open for her son and whispered in his ear as he walked by. "The service has already started, but your father said he's sitting near the front and saved seats for us. Let's try to sit with him."

Jason nodded. Once inside the narthex at the back of the church, he waited for his mother to take the lead. Jason followed his mother down the aisle that divided the nave in half and slipped into the pew beside his father.

Jason's father, Emmanuel, was a large man with black hair and bushy eyebrows that rested on the top of his thin-rimmed glasses like caterpillars. Emmanuel was always well dressed in a suit and tie, and the service tonight was no exception.

Emmanuel leaned toward Jason. "How was the doctor's appointment, son?"

Jason shrugged and wiggled in the pew as he tried to find a comfortable position. "It was okay. I'm in a lot of pain."

Emmanuel rested his large hand on the top of his son's leg. "I am sorry. I will pray that the Lord removes the discomfort," he whispered and turned his attention back to the front of the church where a thin, dark-skinned man was pacing back and forth behind the pulpit.

Jason took the flyer his dad handed him and read the information provided about the visiting pastor. A native of Nigeria, Pastor Chemy had lost many members of his family to wars that ravaged the country. According to the flyer, he still lived in Africa but was in the United States on an evangelism tour, where he was preaching and praying healing over the congregations he visited.

Jason turned his attention to the energetic old man who waved his hands in big circles to illustrate his points. He spoke so loudly that he was almost screaming at times.

He sure is passionate about what he's saying, Jason thought, and as he continued listening to Pastor Chemy, he understood why.

"Forgiveness isn't easy. It isn't natural. When people hurt us, we want to hurt them back. We want to give them a taste of the pain they've inflicted on us," Pastor Chemy said as he looked out at the congregation. "But as Christians, that's not what we're called to do. God wants us to forgive because *we* have been forgiven."

Jason squirmed in his seat, bending and straightening his leg. The pain wasn't any worse, but the pastor's words about the healing of forgiveness were making him uncomfortable. His father looked at him, his eyebrows raised in question.

"Just a little while longer," Emmanuel mouthed the words.

Jason nodded and turned his attention back to the pastor.

"Now if you're like me, you're probably asking yourself 'why should I forgive them when they're not even sorry?' Because let's face it, forgiveness is hard," Pastor Chemy said. "But, I've experienced the freedom that forgiveness brings.

"Nigeria's history is rich in wars. There's fighting among the Nigerian people groups and invasions from outsiders. Many members of my family were killed during these wars, by men I had never met or harmed in any way. For a while I was bitter and angry. After all, who were they to disrupt my life and murder those closest to me?

"It wasn't until after I learned about Jesus and the death he died for the forgiveness of my sins – something I definitely didn't deserve – that I understood how it was possible for me to forgive the men who killed my family. It still wasn't easy, but it was possible.

"Two months after I accepted Jesus, I was presented with the ultimate way of demonstrating forgiveness. The men responsible for my family's deaths were killed in another attack on a village less than a day's walk from mine. One of the men left behind two young daughters..." Pastor Chemy's voice trailed off as he stared up at the ceiling. He closed his eyes and smiled for a full thirty seconds before continuing. "I felt the Lord asking me to demonstrate the reality of my forgiveness by taking care of the orphaned girls, and it was only then that my heart experienced true healing."

Pastor Chemy stepped out from behind the pulpit and descended the altar's stairs. The elderly man moved slowly up the center aisle of the church, singing and praying over the congregation as he walked.

Jason's heart pounded in his chest and his eyes filled with tears as he bowed his head to pray with the pastor. *God, I know this message was for me. I've been harboring bitterness because I don't understand why this injury had to happen to me. It didn't seem fair, and if I'm being honest, it still doesn't. Not really, at least. But if Pastor Chemy could find healing by forgiving the men who killed his family, maybe I can find healing for my hurting heart. I'm sorry for being angry and for doubting that You have my best interest at heart. Please forgive me.*

When he finished praying, Jason opened his eyes and snuck a glance at the other parishioners. Their heads were still bowed, their eyes still closed. As he turned to face the front of the church, Jason noticed that the pain in his leg was completely gone. *That's odd*, he thought. *It must've just left for a little while. The injection probably worked faster today than usual.*

Pastor Chemy completed his tour of the church and returned to the altar. "What you just experienced wasn't me. That was the Holy Spirit working through me to heal. The power of God is what heals His people," Pastor Chemy said. "Let me tell you what the power of God has done in this place. There is a young man here with pain and problems in his left leg that doctors have not been able to fix. Today, God has healed not only his leg but also his heart."

Jason gasped in surprise at the man's words and felt his leg. In total disbelief, he squeezed it, twisted it from side to side, and moved it up and down. As the pastor continued naming others in the congregation who had been healed, Jason looked to his parents in the pew beside him and leaned in to hug them. Their eyes were filled with tears, and the smiles on their faces were evidence of the joy they felt.

Jason refocused his attention on the pastor's words in time to hear him ask for volunteers who would be willing to give a brief testimony. Immediately Jason stood. With tears in his eyes, he handed his cane to his mother and walked unassisted to the front of the church. He cleared his throat and began his story.

"Hello. My name is Jason McGuire. For more than a year I have lived in constant pain because of my RSD, but today, I am completely pain free. God has performed a miracle. He has healed me."

The Man with the Dreads

Luke 4:10 – "For it is written: 'He will command His angels concerning you to guard you carefully;'"

    Leigh Anne pulled the car to the side of the road and parked in front of her parent's house. She pulled the sunshade down, checked her makeup in the mirror, and tucked her short blond hair behind her ears.
    Turning around in the seat to face the boys, she said, "Okay, guys, we're here. You ready?"

Trevor was already standing beside the car, the back door left open in his hurry to retrieve the duffel bags from the trunk.

Sheldon stuffed his headphones into the big pouch of his backpack and zipped it shut. His hair stuck out from under the garnet Carolina baseball cap his father had given him for his ninth birthday last year. The sides of the hat were lined with white salt stains from travel baseball practices under the hot, summer sun.

"I'm ready, Mom," Sheldon said as he opened his door and stepped out into the road.

"Careful, honey. Watch for cars, please," Leigh Anne said, stepping out to join the boys at the trunk.

Trevor set Sheldon's duffel bag on the grass beside the car before grabbing his own. He slammed the trunk closed and slung his bag over his shoulder. He put his arm around Sheldon's shoulder as the boys started up the sidewalk to their grandparent's house.

"Do you guys need help?" Leigh Anne asked as she trailed behind the boys.

"No, ma'am. We're okay," Trevor said without turning his head.

Before Sheldon could knock, the front door swung open and both he and Trevor were engulfed in the large, soft arms of their grandma.

"My boys, I've missed you so much. How are you?" she asked as she held their faces in her warm hands and planted a kiss on their cheeks.

Gran was a short woman, her back stooped with age. Despite being in her late seventies, Gran's short, brown hair curled tightly against her head and held no traces of gray. She grew heavier with each passing holiday but lived with no regrets. Her laughter was contagious, her smile could light up the room, and she knew no stranger.

Sheldon pulled back and wiped his face with the back of his sleeve. "Hi, Gran. We missed you, too. And we're good," he said.

Trevor nodded in agreement. "How are you?"

"Oh, honey, I couldn't be better," she said as she gave them another squeeze. "I'm just so glad to see you both. You've gotten so big."

Sheldon smiled and rolled his eyes. "Gran, you saw us last week. I don't think we've really grown any since then."

Gran wagged her finger at Sheldon, her eyes dancing behind the thick lens of her bifocals. "Don't get smart with me, buster. A grandma knows her grandchildren, and if I say you've grown, you've grown. You'll understand one day."

Sheldon shook his head and looked at Trevor who held his hands up in surrender. "This one's all yours, Sheldon. I'm not about to argue with Gran. She knows her stuff."

Gran laughed. "That's a smart boy, Trevor," she said with a wink. "Y'all run along inside and see if you can help Gramps. I left him upstairs with our suitcases. He might need help bringing them downstairs. Mine's a little heavy."

"Yes, ma'am," Sheldon said as he and Trevor pushed past Gran.

*

Leigh Anne had watched the exchange between her sons and her mother from the bottom of the porch steps. Now she climbed them gingerly and allowed herself to be pulled into her mother's warm embrace.

Gran held Leigh Anne close, rubbing her back rhythmically. After a full minute had passed, Leigh Anne stepped back and looked her mother in the eye, offering a sad smile.

"The boys seem to be handling Sam's uh – " Gran stuttered and lowered her voice, "death well."

Leigh Anne nodded, her eyes moist. She ran a finger under her eyes to catch the tears that threatened to ruin her mascara. "They are," she said quietly.

Gran motioned toward two white, wooden rocking chairs on the covered porch. "Have a minute?" she asked.

Leigh Anne checked her watch and nodded. "I don't have to be anywhere until later tonight. Y'all are the ones with the time crunch," she said.

Gran dismissed the comment with a wave of her hand. "Nonsense. We've got plenty of time. Besides," she paused, "loading my bags in the car will require all three of our guys."

Leigh Anne laughed, despite the sadness of the moment before and settled into the rocker opposite Gran. She leaned back against the wooden slats and looked out over the front yard, dotted with the fresh flower buds that signaled the coming of spring. Leigh Anne sensed her mother watching her and turned to see the woman's bright blue eyes studying her.

Gran spoke softly. "I'm ready to listen when you're ready to talk, honey."

Leigh Anne took a deep breath. "I guess it's just hard, you know? At least harder than I thought that it would be." She paused to gather her thoughts. "I mean, Sam and I weren't married anymore. We had settled our differences, made our peace before we separated five years ago."

Gran nodded, listening, but said nothing.

When Leigh Anne realized her mother wasn't going to speak, she continued. "It's just hard watching my boys suffer." Her voice cracked. "They talked and wrote letters back and forth to their dad when they could, and when Sam was on military leave, he'd spend time with them. Take them camping or to baseball games. To the skate park. They're trying to be strong, probably more for me than for themselves, but I hear them at night, talking and crying. My heart breaks for them." Her voice trailed off.

Gran looked down at her hands, twisting her wedding band on her finger. Finally she spoke. "Well, honey, he *was* still their dad. I think I would be concerned if they weren't sad," she said.

Leigh Anne nodded. "You're right, and I know it." She paused before continuing. "I'm especially worried about Sheldon. He's taking it the hardest. Just last night, after I'd tucked the boys in bed, he came to my room in tears. I asked him what was wrong, and when he finally calmed down enough to answer, you know what he said? He asked, 'Who is going to protect me now?'"

A tear slipped from Leigh Anne's eye and trickled down her cheek. She wiped it away with the back of her hand. "He said, 'I always knew

Dad would watch out for me and that he'd take care of me because he loved me. He was the strongest man in the world.'" Leigh Anne smiled through the sadness.

"And what did you say to him?" Gran asked as she placed her hands on Leigh Anne's shoulders.

"I told him that his father had loved him and Trevor more than anything in this world, and that even though he can't see Sam anymore, he'll be watching over the boys from heaven." Leigh Anne sighed. "To be honest, I don't even know if that's true, but I felt like I had to give him something to hold on to. I don't think there's anything worse than seeing your children in pain and being unable to help them."

Gran smiled, sadness pulling down on the corners of her eyes. "You've got that right," she said.

"And then there's Trevor's newest obsession," Leigh Anne said. She gripped the arms of the rocking chair until her knuckles turned white.

Gran looked at her with raised eyebrows. "Oh? And what might that be?"

"He wants to enlist in the Army, follow in his father's footsteps," Leigh Anne said, her voice rising frantically.

Gran reached over and placed a hand on her daughter's arm. "Honey, you've got to respect his desire to honor his father and protect his country. That kind of sacrifice takes a special person."

"It scares me. What if something happens, like it did to Sam? I can't lose him," Leigh Anne said.

Gran nodded slowly. "I understand that you want to protect him. That's your job as a mother." She paused. "But, that's also several years away. If I remember correctly, he can't enlist until he's seventeen, and even then, he must have parental consent. A lot can happen in between now and then," she said.

Leigh Anne sighed. "You're right. I know you are. It's just been a rollercoaster of a month," she said.

Gran smiled and squeezed her arm. "I know, sweetheart. But look how far they've come already – how far you've all come."

Leigh Anne nodded and returned the squeeze. "You're right, Mom. Thanks for reminding me." She checked her watch. "Where are Gramps and the boys? Y'all need to be getting on the road if you're going to make it to the cabin before dark."

"Is that my Annie?" a deep voice came from the doorway behind her.

Leigh Anne turned to see her dad emerge from the house, one large duffel bag slung over his shoulder and another being pulled behind him. The boys followed him onto the porch, still carrying their overnight bags. They hopped down the steps and raced to the driveway, stopping beside their grandparents' car.

At six foot four inches, Leigh Anne's father had always been larger than life on many levels. He was kind and compassionate, protecting her mother and her sisters fiercely. A successful, respected manager at his engineering firm, her father had learned the delicate balance between home and family, mastering it with ease.

"Hi, Daddy," Leigh Anne said as she rose and planted a quick kiss on his cheek. "Can I help you with something?"

"I've got these bags," he said. "But if you wanted to open the trunk for me, I wouldn't turn that down."

"Of course. Where is the key?" she asked.

Gran fished the key from her pocket and held it out to Leigh Anne, who stepped gingerly from the porch and jogged ahead of her father and the boys to her parents' white Cadillac sedan. The car beeped when Leigh Anne clicked the unlock button, and she lifted the trunk before backing away to allow her dad access to the space.

Gramps tossed the bags into the empty trunk and wiped the sweat from his brow with the sleeve of his striped button down shirt. "Whew. Gran, next time we plan a weekend trip to the mountains, try not to pack the entire closet and bathroom," he said, winking at the boys who stifled chuckles.

"When you realize you've forgotten something, don't come crying to me," Gran said as she brushed past him with another bag and her purse. She set them in the floorboard of the passenger seat before straightening up and making a show of brushing her hands off in front of her.

"Don't worry, I won't," Gramps said under his breath, just loud enough for Leigh Anne to hear.

She pursed her lips, refusing to giggle aloud and feed the friendly squabble between her parents.

"What was that?" Gran said as she walked over to join the others.

When no one answered, she turned to Gramps. "Don't get me started. I can make this trip seem as short or long as I'd like. Remember that, buster," she said, poking her finger into his chest.

"Yes, dear," Gramps conceded. Turning to the boys, he said, "Throw your bags in the back, guys. Let's get this show on the road!"

Trevor and Sheldon tossed their duffel bags into the trunk and packed them down around their grandmother's things. Trevor gave his mom a quick hug and kiss on the cheek before running around the car to the back seat and climbing inside.

Sheldon took his hat off and gave Leigh Anne a long hug, squeezing her tightly as he rested his head on her shoulder. "Are you sure you can't come with us tonight?" he asked.

Leigh Anne ran her fingers through his smooth blond hair. "I'm sure, honey, but I'll be there tomorrow afternoon. You'll have a great time tonight with Gran and Gramps and Trevor," she said.

Sheldon nodded, his bottom lip sticking out in disappointment.

Leigh Anne tried again. "Plus, I think you're meeting Aunt Cindy, Uncle David and the girls for dinner on the way. They'll follow y'all to the cabin tonight."

Sheldon's eyes lit up. "I didn't know they were coming tonight, too. That sounds kinda fun," he said, a lopsided grin spreading across his face.

Leigh Anne gave Sheldon one last quick hug and pushed him toward the car door. "It'll be a blast. Tell me all about it when I get there tomorrow, okay?"

Sheldon nodded and climbed in the car.

Gramps wrapped his strong arms around Leigh Anne and kissed the top of her head. She relaxed in the safety of his embrace. "Thanks for taking the boys up with you for me tonight. They need to remember what it's like to be happy, and this is just the thing. Thank you," she said, meaning it.

Gramps nodded and squeezed her tightly. "We all do. See you tomorrow, sweetheart?"

Leigh Anne nodded and handed Gramps the car keys. He climbed into the driver's seat and started the engine. Leigh Anne stepped onto the grass, clearing a path down the driveway to the road. She waved to her parents and her sons as the car backed out of the driveway and turned out of the neighborhood before she climbed into her own car and drove away.

*

"Gramps, you're swerving into the other lane," Sheldon said from the seat behind his grandfather.

Gramps tightened his grip on the steering wheel and straightened in his seat. Gran looked at him from the passenger seat, concern deepening the lines around her eyes.

"Are you okay, dear?" she asked. "If you're tired, I can drive."

Gramps shook his head. "It's not me. It's the car. Do you feel how bumpy it is?" he asked.

Gran nodded.

"I think something's wrong with one of the tires," Gramps said.

Gran gasped. "Oh, no. Do you need to pull over?"

"I will when we stop for dinner. The Chick-fil-a we're meeting Cindy, David, and the girls at is just ahead, right?" he asked.

Gran nodded. "Yes. About a mile down the road."

"Good. I'll look at it there," Gramps said. "We should be just fine."

Gran settled back into her seat and glanced at the boys in the backseat. Sheldon looked out the window at the passing cars and the sun as it reflected on the lake beside the road while Trevor's head was buried in his hand-held gaming system.

Sheldon turned and saw his grandmother's eyes watching him. He smiled and waved, removing the headphones from his ears. "Is something wrong, Gran?" he asked.

"No, dear. I was just thinking," she said.

"Oh," Sheldon hesitated. "Thinking is good, I guess. Are we almost there?"

"I'm afraid not, son," Gramps said before his wife could reply.

"Why not? It seems like we've been driving for hours. I'm starving!" Sheldon whined.

"We're not *almost* there because we *are* here," Gramps said with a laugh as he turned the car into the parking lot and eased into a vacant parking space, delineated by fading white paint. A band of cars waiting in the drive-thru line wrapped around the building, while other vehicles filled almost every parking space in the lot. "And how can you be starving? Your mom said you ate lunch right before she dropped you off at our house. That was two hours ago."

"Finally!" Sheldon exclaimed. "And I'm a growing boy, so I'm always hungry. Do you think Aunt Cindy and Uncle David and the girls are already here?"

Gran smiled. "I don't see their car, but I'm sure they will be soon. Why don't we go inside and wait in line, okay? Maybe we'll be at the front of the line when they get here so we can all order together," she said.

Sheldon and Trevor climbed out of the car and waited by the hood for their grandparents to join them. Gramps opened the door for his wife, stealing a kiss as she stood and joined the boys.

"Y'all go ahead," Gramps said. "I'm going to take a look at the tires while there's no one parked beside us. I'll be right there."

*

An hour later, Sheldon piled into the backseat with a stomach full of chicken and waffle fries. Trevor climbed in behind him, an unfinished milkshake still in in his hand.

"Careful, Trevor. I don't want cookies and cream milkshake all over my iPod or Beats," Sheldon warned.

"I am being careful. There's hardly any left anyway. See?" Trevor said as he slurped the last traces of milkshake from the Styrofoam cup.

"Easy, fellows," Gran said. "I know you're getting tired and restless, but we'll be to the cabin soon. Only about an hour left now."

"Whew, I'm glad we're almost there," Sheldon said. "I'm a little tired of being stuck in the car."

"I know you are, dear. I am, too," Gran said. "All this sitting is hard on the old bones."

"You're not old, Gran. You're just," he hesitated, searching for the right word, "mature. Yes, that's it. You're just mature," Sheldon said matter-of-factly.

Gran and Gramps laughed. "Mature, huh? Have you seen your grandmother dance around the house while she cleans? I think you have the wrong woman," Gramps said, teasing.

Gran swatted her husband gently on the arm. "Hey, now. That's not dancing, that's exercising. I'm killing two birds with one stone." She turned around and winked at her grandson. "And multi-tasking is *very* mature," she finished.

Sheldon nodded. "Yeah, Gramps. You have to be very mature to multi-task. I can't even eat breakfast and watch cartoons at the same time in the mornings before school. I forget to eat."

Gramps chuckled. "I'm sure one day you'll master the art," he said. Buckling his seatbelt, he focused on driving.

"Everybody ready?" Gramps asked.

"Wait, are Aunt Cindy and the others following us?" Sheldon asked.

"Yes, dear. They'll be right behind us the whole way," Gran said. Turning to her husband, she asked, "Did you check the tires? Is everything okay?"

He nodded, his brow furrowed. "Nothing seemed to be wrong with any of them. If I notice something again, we'll pull over and call someone, okay?"

Gran nodded, satisfied.

Gramps pulled out of the parking space and circled the restaurant slowly, giving his daughter and her family time to fall in line behind him. He turned out of the parking lot and eased onto the on ramp before picking up speed and merging on the interstate.

Gran checked the side mirrors. "Honey, I don't see Cindy's car. Should we pull over and wait?"

"They'll catch up soon enough. We're just traveling interstate the rest of the way," Gramps said.

Gran nodded, her face still clouded with concern.

Gramps reached for her hand and gave it a gentle squeeze. "If you're worried about them, give her a call," he suggested.

"I don't want to distract them. I just don't see their car," Gran said.

"I'm sure they're back there," Gramps said. "The interstate is pretty busy for four in the afternoon. I think we're still ahead of rush hour traffic, but it's not as empty as I expected. They probably got stuck behind a slower car," he reassured her.

Gran nodded and pulled a magazine out of her purse. She flipped a few pages to an article about a healing relationship between a therapy dog and a young boy with autism. She stopped reading when she felt a pat on her arm. Turning around in the seat, she saw her grandson staring at her, his eyes wide in fear.

"What's wrong, Sheldon?" she asked.

"Do you feel that?" Sheldon asked.

She shook her head slowly and cast a cursory glance at her husband who shrugged. "No, dear. What should I be feeling?" she asked.

"There is it again. That bumping," Sheldon said. "What is it?"

"I did feel it that time," Gramps said. "I'll pull over at the next exit. I checked the tires but couldn't see anything wrong with them."

Gramps looked at his wife. "Call Cindy, would you? Tell her we're going to pull off at the next exit. Ask them to do the same. I want David to take a look at the car and see if I missed something."

Gran nodded and set her purse on her lap, feeling around for her cell phone. When she found it, she dropped the bag to the floor and unlocked the screen to search her contacts for her daughter's number. Just before Gran pressed the green call button, a loud noise like a gunshot echoed through the car. Gran looked at her husband, his knuckles white as he gripped the steering wheel, his face drawn up in fear.

The rear of the car swerved back and forth over the white lines as Gramps tried to maintain control of the car. As it spun toward the side of the road, Gramps yelled, "Everybody, hold on!" as the car careened off the road, flipping several times before it came to a rest on its side.

*

Sheldon's eyes fluttered open, and he blinked several times, trying to clear the blurriness that was clouding his vision. As his eyes scanned his surroundings, he realized that everything seemed to be sideways. Sheldon shook his head quickly and squeezed his eyes shut, but when he opened them again, everything still looked strange.

Where am I? And why is everything sideways? Sheldon wondered.

He looked down and saw a seat belt pulled tightly across his chest and wrapped around his body. He tried to sit up but the thick belt held him tightly, dangling in midair. Suddenly, he remembered everything. Tires squealing, the vehicle flipping, glass shattering, and the piercing wail of his grandmother's cry.

"Gran? Gramps? Trevor?" Sheldon called, quietly at first. "Is anyone there?" When his cries were met with silence, Sheldon yelled louder. "Help! Gramps! Trevor! I'm stuck in the car!"

He waited but heard nothing but the sound of sirens wailing in the distance. Sheldon fought to remain calm, but between his racing heart and his throbbing head, all he could think about was how he wished his father was there to save him. He struggled against the seat belt, but he couldn't dislodge himself from the tangle of material. He gave up, defeated.

"Dad," he croaked. "None of this would've happened if you were here."

Sheldon pounded his fist against the side of the car and let the tears come. When he felt a cool breeze filter into the car and rustle his hair, Sheldon's heart dropped. He placed his hand on his head, already knowing that his dad's hat wasn't there. He scanned the floorboard of the car and craned his neck to look into the front half of the car, but it was useless. The car was a mess. Leftover drinks, toys, and his grandmother's magazines lined every inch of the interior of the car. Sheldon noticed splatters of red on the front windshield but quickly looked away, not wanting to consider what it could mean.

Sheldon heard the crunching of shoes on gravel and turned to look behind him. The car's back window had been shattered in the wreck, leaving shards of glass spiking haphazardly out at all angles.

"I'm in here," Sheldon called out, his voice just barely above a whisper.

A head appeared on the other side of the window. Sheldon gasped and shrank back against the seat belt. He didn't recognize the face that stared back at him. Sheldon watched from the shadows as the man stuck his head through the opening that had been the rear windshield.

"Hello? I thought I heard somebody in here?" the voice said, strong and sure.

"I'm over here," Sheldon said, lifting his hand in a small wave.

The man smiled, his white teeth standing out against the darkening sky of dusk. The man squeezed through the opening as glass shards pulled at his white t-shirt and the long black dreads that hung around his face and trailed down his back.

"There you are, little dude," the man said as he eased into the car and stopped beside Sheldon.

When the man placed a hand on the boy's shoulder, Sheldon felt the rough skin of his fingers through his shirt. The man studied the seat belt then asked, "What do you say we get you out of here?"

Sheldon nodded. "Yes, sir, please."

"You don't need to 'sir' me," the man said with a chuckle, his large hands already unwinding the seat belt from its grip on Sheldon's small body.

Less than a minute later, Sheldon was free and following the man as he climbed across the back seat toward the rear windshield.

"Let me go first. Then I'll help you out," the man said as he slid through the opening. His shirt hooked on a piece of glass, creating a tear a couple inches long. He reached back and slipped the cloth off the glass before snaking his legs through the maze of glass. When he was through the opening, the man bent down in front of the hole. "Okay, Sheldon. It's your turn. You ready?"

Sheldon nodded and swallowed past the lump that had formed in his throat. He was afraid that the shards of glass would cut him as he climbed through the hole.

"Give me your hands," the man said, reaching his own out toward the boy.

Sheldon did as he was asked, and the man pulled him through the hole in one swift movement, setting the boy carefully on the ground. The man stood and brushed his hands on his jeans.

"You okay?" he asked.

Sheldon scanned his arms and legs for cuts or bruises. Finding none, he nodded. "Yes, sir. Thank you, sir."

The man lowered himself onto one knee so he was eye level with the boy. "Your grandparents are over there," the man said as he pointed to a crowd of EMTs swarming around two ambulances. "They're a little beaten up, but they'll be okay."

"What about my brother?" Sheldon asked.

The man smiled. "He's just fine. He and your aunt are actually looking for you," the man said as he stood. "You should probably go find them. They're worried about you."

Sheldon nodded. "Yes, sir. I will." He turned to leave.

"Wait, son. I think you're forgetting something."

Sheldon stopped at the man's voice and turned to face him. "I am?"

The man smiled and pulled Sheldon's garnet baseball cap out from behind his back. "You might want to hang onto this. I heard someone pretty special gave it to you."

Sheldon took the cap from the man and turned it over in his hands in amazement. "Wow. Thank you, sir. My dad gave me this hat," Sheldon paused, remembering the day his dad had given him the hat. "You know what he said?"

The man didn't speak but raised an eyebrow in question.

"He said that even if he wasn't around, as long as I was wearing the hat, he'd be with me."

"Then I guess it's a good thing I noticed the hat in the floorboard of the car," the man said. "Now run along. Your family is looking for you."

Sheldon took off toward the parade of police cars and ambulances that lined the side of the highway. Their sirens had quieted, but the red and blue lights still flashed brightly against the darkening sky. He saw his aunt and brother sitting on the grassy embankment twenty feet from the interstate and called out to them as he approached.

"Trevor! Aunt Cindy!"

At the sound of Sheldon's voice, his aunt and brother stood. As they ran to meet him, an EMT grabbed Sheldon's shoulder.

"Are you the boy who was still in the car?" the EMT asked. He wore light blue scrubs, and his hands were covered with latex gloves.

Sheldon nodded.

"We were just coming back for you. Are you okay? Come with me and let's go check you out," the EMT urged.

Sheldon wiggled away from the man's grip. "No, sir. I'm okay. I need to see my family," he said as he ran the rest of the way to meet his aunt and brother.

"Sheldon! There you are. Are you okay? We've been looking all over for you," Aunt Cindy said as she engulfed the boy in her arms.

Sheldon pushed his aunt's long brown hair out of his face. "I was stuck in the back of the car, but I'm okay. A nice man helped me get out. Where are Gran and Gramps? Are they okay?" he asked.

"Yes, Gran and Gramps will be just fine. They have a few cuts and scrapes, but they are being cared for by the EMTs over at the ambulances. Are you hurt?" she asked, holding

Sheldon at arms' length and examining him for scratches or breaks.

"No, I'm fine," Sheldon said. He turned to his brother who was crying. "Are you hurt?"

Trevor shook his head and wiped his nose with the back of his sleeve. "No, I'm okay."

"Then why are you crying?" Sheldon asked.

"I shouldn't have left you in the car," Trevor said, reaching out to hug his little brother. "I guess I was so shaken up by the wreck that I didn't think about anything except getting out of the car, so I crawled out where the window used to be," he said as fresh tears sprang to his eyes. "How could I have been so dumb? I can't believe I left without looking for you. I'm so sorry."

"It's really okay," Sheldon said nonchalantly. "You weren't thinking straight. I'm fine, so no harm done." He patted Trevor on the back.

Trevor took a deep breath, trying to stop the hiccups that racked his thin frame. "Wait. How did you say you got out again? A man helped you?"

Sheldon nodded, his eyes scanning the area for the large, kind stranger who had rescued him. "Yeah. The man with the dreads helped me out of the car."

Sheldon watched Trevor and his aunt exchange glances, their eyebrows knitted together in confusion. Trevor shrugged, and Aunt Cindy shook her head at a loss for words.

"What man with dreads, honey?" Aunt Cindy finally asked, as she too searched the crowd of bystanders and witnesses for a man meeting Sheldon's description.

"I forgot to ask him what his name was before I came to find you. He told me y'all were looking for me. You haven't seen him?" Sheldon asked. When Trevor and Aunt Cindy shook their heads, Sheldon continued, his voice almost a whisper. "That's weird. He was just here."

"How exactly did he help you?" Trevor asked.

"When the car finally stopped flipping, my side of the car was in the air. I was stuck in my seat, hanging from the seatbelt. I couldn't get out and was really scared." He paused, gathering his thoughts. "The next thing I knew, a man with dreads stuck his head in the hole where the back window used to be. He told me not to worry because he had come to cut me out of the seatbelt. He even knew my name," Sheldon finished.

"So the man with the dreads saved you?" Trevor asked.

Sheldon nodded. "Yeah."

"What happened after he got you out of the car?" Trevor asked.

"Nothing really. He told me to come find you because you were looking for me," Sheldon said. After a moment's pause he continued, "Oh, and he gave me my hat back. It must've fallen off in the wreck."

"Where'd he go?" Trevor asked.

Sheldon scratched his head and shrugged. "I don't know. I didn't watch to see. I was focused on finding y'all."

"Well he couldn't have just disappeared. He has to be around here somewhere," Trevor said, reaching for his brother's hand.

"I don't know, Trevor. I don't see him anywhere," Sheldon replied. "Trust me, I'd know him if I saw him."

Just then a uniformed police officer walked by. Sheldon hesitated and pulled back against his brother, stepping out and placing a hand on the officer's arm. The officer glanced down at the boy. "Yes? Can I help you?"

"Um, yes, sir," Sheldon stammered. "I was wondering if you've seen a tall man with dreadlocks? He's wearing jeans and a white t-shirt."

The officer's brow furrowed in confusion. "No, son, I haven't seen him. But we've asked all bystanders to return to their cars and leave the vicinity. It's an unnecessary risk having these extra bodies milling around so close to the interstate." Without another word, the officer turned and walked away.

Sheldon cast one last look over his shoulder toward the crowd that had gathered over the past hour. Police officers were dispersing the bystanders, herding them back to their vehicles.

Trevor turned to Sheldon. "Are you sure you saw the man right? Maybe you weren't paying as close attention as you thought."

Sheldon shook his head vehemently. "No. I know what I saw. The man with the dreads saved me, but I don't understand how he could've disappeared into thin air. It just doesn't make sense."

Trevor shrugged and crossed his arms. "I don't know, little brother. It *is* pretty strange," he said. He saw his aunt out of the corner of his eye. "Aunt Cindy, are you okay?"

Sheldon followed Trevor's gaze and let his eyes rest on his aunt, whose eyes were wide and mouth hung open. The color had drained from her face. "Aunt Cindy?" he echoed.

Aunt Cindy closed her mouth and nodded slowly. "Boys, God is always watching out for His children. Sometimes He sends angels to protect us, and sometimes He just wants to remind us that He cares for us," she said as she placed her arms on each of her nephews' shoulders. She looked from one boy to the other. "I think Sheldon's friend was one of those angels."

Just Go

Jeremiah 33:3 – "Call to me and I will answer you and tell you great and unsearchable things you do not know."

Greg flipped on the car's blinker and looked over his shoulder before easing into the lane to his right. He checked the clock on the dash. 6:02. He sighed. With rush hour traffic, he was still a good twenty minutes from the small upstairs apartment he and his wife, Melissa, rented from Seth and Nancy Little, an elderly couple in their fifty-fifth year of marriage, while they finished their programs of study at Covenant College.

Greg's mind played through the list of class assignments due in the upcoming weeks as he sought to finish the courses required for his ministerial degree before May graduation rolled around. Convinced that he wasn't forgetting any important deadlines in the next few days, Greg relaxed his grip on the steering wheel and settled back into the worn leather seat. Upon resting his head against the tattered headrest, he felt the sharp edges of the weathered leather poke his scalp through his short, thinning brown hair. He pulled the visor down to block the setting sun and squinted against the brightness of the rays as he merged onto the road that would lead him to the top of Lookout Mountain.

As Greg leaned forward to adjust the radio dial, the cell phone in his back pocket vibrated. He pulled it out and saw Melissa's name on the screen. He smiled.

"Hi, sweetheart," Greg said.

"Hi, Greg." His wife's soft voice sounded even quieter on the phone than in person. "Where are you?"

"I got held up at the office this afternoon. I'm on deadline for a class assignment, and then Pastor Dyson wanted to speak with me before I left, but I'm on my way now. Is everything okay?" he asked.

"Oh." His wife's monosyllabic answer heightened his concern.

Melissa rarely called just to talk. She was one of the few women he knew who hated talking on the phone, and she had been that way for as long as he could remember. *Please let nothing be wrong*, he thought.

"Honey, what's wrong?" Greg asked.

"Nothing. Well, everything," Melissa said, her voice cracking and her words giving way to quiet sobs.

"Sweetheart, I need you to take a deep breath and talk to me. Please tell me what's the matter," Greg coaxed. "Whatever is bothering you, we can fix it, darling. But I can't help if I don't know what's wrong."

He heard Melissa hiccup and draw a long, slow breath. Her voice shook when she said, "I let the casserole for dinner burn." He heard her voice catch as she steadied her voice and continued. "I know you're under so much pressure at school. Plus, your responsibilities at the church take up so much time. I just wanted to surprise you with a quiet night at home, your favorite meal by candlelight and maybe a movie afterward. I guess I could go to the store and get more ingredients for another casserole, but that would push dinner back until almost ten. So now I'm not sure what to do."

Greg closed his eyes in relief as his wife rambled on about ways to save the evening, but opened them again when the car behind him honked. He jerked the steering wheel, guiding the car back between the white lines on his side of the road.

"Is that all? The burnt casserole is the sole reason for the tears?" Greg asked, trying to hide the relief he felt for fear that his wife would think he was taking the situation too lightly. Lately she had been more sensitive, and the last thing he wanted was an argument over the phone.

"Yes, that's all. I know it could be much worse. I just wanted a perfect night with you. If we were home, I could even call Mom. She'd have cooked extra food like always and would invite us over, covering for my mistake. But home's several hours away, and I don't know what to do about dinner now." She paused and added, "I'm sorry."

"Sweetheart, it's okay," Greg said, searching for the right words to console his bride. "I tell you what. Go change into something comfortable and grab a blanket. I'll pick you up in five minutes. We'll grab a pizza and take it to the park for a picnic, okay?"

*

Half an hour later, Greg parked the car in the gravel lot beside the park at the top of Lookout Mountain. He climbed out of the driver's seat and ran around the car to open the door for Melissa. She was tall and thin, with thick brown hair that draped over her shoulders. Greg watched her bright blue eyes follow him as he ran around the car. When he pretended to hit his knee against the front bumper, she laughed, a sound that still made his heart skip a beat.

Melissa handed him the pizza box. "Careful. The bottom's still hot," she said as she reached over the center console to grab the red-and blue-checkered blanket from the backseat.

Greg reached for her hand. The gravel scattered under their feet as he led her across the parking lot to a grassy field surrounded by tall oak trees. Melissa handed him two corners of the blanket. Taking the others in her hands, she spread the blanket on the grass, crawling across it to smooth out the wrinkles.

When Melissa stopped in the middle of the blanket and crossed her legs in front of her, Greg sat down beside his wife, placing the pizza box on the blanket between them. Melissa pulled two bottles of water out of her purse, keeping one and handing the other to him.

"This is the blanket from the day I proposed!" Greg exclaimed as he ran his hand across the blanket's picked fleece. He smiled, remembering the afternoon he got down on one knee amid the reds and yellows and oranges of the changing seasons at the top of Lookout Mountain. "You thought of everything," Greg said, leaning in to kiss his wife on the cheek.

Melissa smiled. "I tried. I wanted to make sure you knew how much I love you, how proud I am of you. It was the least I could do after ruining dinner," she said, her lip protruding in a fake pout.

Greg gently placed a finger against her lips. "Shh, none of that," he said as he unscrewed the top of his water bottle. After taking a sip, he continued, "This is better anyway. You love picnics. Besides, this is a pretty great place, don't you think?"

Melissa laughed. "You always know just what to say, and yes, this is one of my favorite spots in the world. The man of my dreams asked me to marry him just over there," she said, pointing to a bench shrouded in trees on the other side of the field.

"I know," Greg said. "The best part was that I only had to wait a few months before I actually got to marry you."

"I loved that we were able to get married at New Hope Church and that my grandfather could preside over the ceremony. As if I didn't already feel like a princess, those things made the wedding that much more magical," she said with a sigh.

Greg nodded his agreement. "There was something special about sharing the greatest moment of my life with the people at home." His voice trailed off and he grew quiet, remembering the moment two years ago that changed his life forever.

"Hey, are you okay?" Melissa asked. She placed her hand on his shoulder, her brow drawn in concern. "You spaced out on me a little there."

Greg nodded, trying to gather his thoughts. "Could I tell you something?" He took her small hands in his own.

"Yes, of course," Melissa stuttered. "You can always tell me everything."

Greg took a deep breath. "The reason I was late coming home today?" he began.

"You said you had a meeting with Pastor Dyson."

Pastor Dyson, the senior pastor at Mount Chapel Baptist Church, was a round man with a big heart. Despite his wife's premature death over thirty years ago, Pastor Dyson had not remarried, choosing instead to devote his life to the church. Though his waistline had expanded and his body wore down more with each passing year, his mind remained as sharp as ever.

Greg nodded. "I was packing up to come home for the day when he knocked on my office door and entered the room. He asked if we could talk for a minute, so of course I said yes. I figured he wanted to talk about one of the kids in the youth group." He paused before continuing. "But I was wrong."

"What did he want to talk to you about?" Melissa asked, the creases in her forehead deepening.

"He offered me the associate pastor position at church!" Greg exclaimed.

Melissa's eyes grew wide, a smile spread across her face. "You're kidding!" she said.

Greg shook his head. "No, honey, not at all. If I want the job, it's all mine following graduation in December. Pastor Dyson said he's impressed with what I've done with the youth ministry and can't think of anyone better to lead the congregation with him."

Melissa flung her thin frame toward her husband, wrapping her arms around his neck. "Oh my gosh! That's wonderful!" She planted a kiss on his cheek and pulled back to look him in the eyes. "I'm so proud of you!"

Greg smiled, pulling her into a hug. "Thanks, sweetheart. It still seems a little surreal to me," he said.

"Well, it doesn't surprise me," she said.

"It doesn't?" Greg asked. "Why not?"

Melissa returned to her spot on the blanket, opened the cardboard pizza box, and grabbed a slice of pizza. She took a bite, a string of cheese dangling from her mouth as she spoke. "Because Pastor Dyson finally realized what I've known all along," she said matter-of-factly.

Greg reached for the cheese on his wife's chin, smiling as her face turned red. "And what have you known all along?" he asked.

"That you are one of the most godly men around." Melissa took another bite of pizza. "But I've got one up on Pastor Dyson. I get to call you my husband."

*

As the final chords of the offertory song echoed through the old chapel, Greg and Melissa slipped out of the pew they shared with his parents and headed for the back of the building.

Built in the early 1900s, the chapel was small and lacked the elaborate crosses and colors of modern churches. When the small wooden chapel was constructed, a single stained glass window had been installed in the wall behind the pulpit. The window contained pieces of glass in various shades of reds, blues, greens, and yellows and depicted the parable of Jesus feeding the multitude with just five loaves of bread and two fish. The story reminded Greg that God is faithful to provide, and the window had always been his favorite part of the building because when the sun's rays filtered through the glass, a rainbow of colored light danced on the gray carpet of the chapel.

Despite their early departure and attempt to disappear out the back and to the parking lot without being noticed, the couple was stopped in the foyer by several old friends. While Melissa made small talk with a few girls she cheered with during high school, Greg shook hands and slapped the backs of several of his football teammates from the glory days. He kept glancing at his wife, waiting for her cue that it was time to leave.

Melissa's parents had invited the couple to join them for lunch after church, before they left to return to Covenant later in the day. Greg knew Melissa was eager to see her parents. She had always been a homebody, and there had been times, especially early in their marriage, when he had been woken by her quiet sobs of missing home in the middle of the night. Though those days were past, Melissa still craved time with her family, a luxury often overlooked amid the busyness of college and married life.

As Melissa excused herself from the conversation with her friends and pulled Greg toward the chapel doors, the senior pastor of New Hope Church, Dr. Travis Johnson, came up behind them. The pastor was a large man, solidly built from playing collegiate football. His short brown hair was thinning with age, and wire-rimmed glasses framed his gray eyes.

"Greg," Pastor Johnson said, placing a hand on the young man's shoulder. "Could I speak with you for a minute?"

Greg looked at Melissa, raising his eyebrows in question. She nodded and smiled despite the disappointment he sensed she was feeling at the proposed delay.

Turning back to Pastor Johnson, Greg nodded. "Sure, Pastor. I'd be happy to talk for a moment."

Greg leaned in to kiss his wife. "Why don't you go ahead and start the car? I'll be right there."

"Actually, I was hoping I could speak with both of you," Pastor Johnson said.

"Oh, of course, Pastor," Greg said, placing his hand on the small of Melissa's back.

"Wonderful. Let's step into my office for a moment. I'm sure you have places to go and people to see while you're home. I won't hold you long," Pastor Johnson said as he led them to a solid wood door at back of the chapel.

The pastor's office was conservatively decorated, a reflection of his simplistic taste. An old computer and picture of his family sat atop a large wooden desk situated in the corner of the room. A tall bookshelf stood beside the solitary office window that looked out on the church parking lot. Several paintings of Biblical events hung in gold frames on the walls, and two mismatched chairs faced the desk.

"Please. Take a seat," Pastor Johnson said, motioning for the couple to sit in the chairs. He closed the door and took a seat in the chair behind his desk. When everyone was situated, he continued. "Like I said, I'll keep this brief as I'm sure your families are expecting to spend time with you this afternoon."

Greg nodded. He reached for Melissa's hand and gave it a gentle squeeze.

"Greg, it's my understanding that you'll graduate with a ministry degree in December?" Pastor Johnson asked.

"Yes, sir, barring some unforeseen circumstance, that's the plan," Greg said.

"You'll graduate then as well?" Pastor Johnson directed the question to Melissa, who nodded.

Pastor Johnson smiled and closed his eyes momentarily. When he reopened them, he spoke pointedly. "If you don't mind me asking, what are your plans following graduation? Will you stay somewhere in Georgia or return home here to South Carolina?"

Greg looked at Melissa. She smiled and raised her eyebrows, waiting for his response. This was the question that had plagued him for months.

"I wish I could tell you, Pastor," Greg drew a deep breath. "Truth is, we're not sure yet. I've been offered the position of associate pastor at our church in Georgia, and while I'm grateful for that, I also know that my wife would love to move back home." He looked at Melissa and winked. "We're hoping to have some little ones on the way in the next few years, and we'd both like for our children to grow up around family."

Pastor Johnson leaned forward in his chair and rested his elbows on his desk. "Yes, I see," he said slowly. "I'm going to cut to the chase. New Hope is in need of a youth minister. The number of middle and high school students in the congregation is growing at an overwhelming rate, and we have sufficient funds to hire someone to work solely with the youth. I've heard about your success with the kids in Georgia and would love to partner with someone like you in ministry, though it seems that I may be too late with my offer."

Greg covered his mouth with his hand as he sat speechlessly staring from the pastor to his wife. "What exactly are you saying?" he asked as he fought to keep his mind from spinning.

Pastor Johnson smiled. "I'd like to offer you the opportunity to serve as the first youth pastor in the history of New Hope Church."

*

Greg pulled to the side of the road and parked the car in front of the house he and Melissa rented. He grabbed his backpack from the passenger seat and locked the car before stuffing his gloved hands in the pockets of his trench coat. He could see the puffs of his breath in the frigid evening air as he jogged up the sidewalk and around the house to the back entrance that led directly to their second floor apartment.

He unlocked the door to the narrow staircase and bounded up the steps two at a time. Pushing the door open, he was greeted by the kitchen's warmth and the aroma of vegetable stew.

"Hi, honey. How was your day?" Melissa said. She smiled at him from where she stood by the sink, the lower half of her arms covered in soap bubbles as she washed the pile of dishes that had accumulated over the past few days. Greg couldn't suppress the smile that formed on his lips as he looked at his beautiful bride. Even wearing a stained apron and with her hair pulled back in a ponytail, the sight of her made his palms clammy.

"It's a lot better now that I'm here with you," he said, leaning in to kiss her on the cheek.

She laughed, the melodic sound causing his heart to skip a beat.

"You're too much sometimes. Do you know that?" she asked.

He shrugged. "I'm hoping that's a good thing? Let me put my things away and I'll help you finish dinner."

Greg dropped his backpack on the floor in the living room and grabbed a t-shirt and pair of sweatpants from a basket of unfolded clothes in the laundry room. He changed and ran a brush through his hair before returning to the kitchen.

"I'm back and reporting for duty," Greg said, sneaking up behind his wife and wrapping his arms around her waist.

She jumped, startled by the sound of his voice, but relaxed into his embrace, leaning her head back against his chest. "Would you rather wash or dry?" she asked.

"I'll dry," Greg said, grabbing the dishtowel that hung from the oven handle.

He picked up a plate from the dish rack and ran the towel over the porcelain before setting it on the marble countertop and selecting another plate. His mind raced as he went over his mental list of class assignments due in the coming days, finally settling on the ministry decision he had to make by the end of next week.

"You're awfully quiet tonight," Melissa said.

Greg looked up and set the plate and towel on the counter. Crossing his arms, he leaned against the refrigerator for support. "I talked to Pastor Dyson today. I told him about the job offer at New Hope," he said.

Melissa turned the faucet off and shook the water from her hands, drying them on her apron. "What did he say?" she asked.

Greg sighed. "He seemed genuinely happy for me."

"That doesn't surprise me," Melissa said. "He's a God-fearing man with the purest intentions."

"It didn't surprise me either," Greg said. "He advised me to pray about the decision and remain true to my convictions, but said that he would need an answer soon so that the church could start the process of searching for another candidate to fill my place should I choose not to stay at Mount Lookout."

"What exactly does 'soon' mean?" Melissa asked.

The oven timer beeped, signaling that the stew had finished cooking. She grabbed an oven mitt, opened the door, and lifted the stew onto the stove.

"He gave me until the end of November," Greg said. He watched his wife nod, her eyes suddenly growing wide.

"The end of November? That's next Friday!" she exclaimed.

"I know. It doesn't seem like a lot of time, but Pastor Dyson's right. I owe it to both churches to make my decision so that they can nominate a search committee and move forward," Greg said, running his hand through his hair.

Melissa flipped the oven off and walked across the kitchen. She wrapped her hands around his waist and laid her head against his chest. Greg closed his eyes and breathed in the smell of her lavender shampoo.

"What do you think you're going to do?" she murmured into his t-shirt.

Greg let out a long sigh. "I'm going to do a lot of praying and seeking God. I want to know what His will for us is. Because in this case both options are good, I want to know His *specific* will – I want to know which job He desires me to take." He paused. "This one's hard because I usually know exactly what to do. I fix things. But this time I don't want to do what is easy. I want to do what is right, you know?"

Melissa nodded and lifted her clear blue eyes to his. "I want that, too." Her eyes filled with tears until one by one they trickled down her cheek.

Greg wiped them away with his finger, his heart breaking. "Don't cry, sweetheart. Can you tell me what's wrong?" he asked, already knowing the heart of the answer.

Melissa took a deep breath. "I need you to know something," she said, stepping back and gripping his arms with her long, thin fingers.

Greg nodded, waiting breathlessly for his wife's words.

"*I* want you to take the job back home. I'm ready to be near family. But when I became your wife," she paused, blinking back tears, "I made the commitment to follow you wherever you go and to submit to your decisions, so long as they align with God's standards. I need you to know that I will do that," Melissa said, her voice cracking with emotion.

Greg felt a tear slip down his cheek as he pulled close the woman he loved. *Thank you, God, for this gift. May I never take her for granted.*

*

"Greg! Over here," a familiar voice called from the other side of the parking lot.

Greg popped the trunk of his car and climbed out of the driver's seat to see his friend, Tim, walking toward him. Three years ago, Tim and Greg had met in their freshman English class at Covenant, and Greg soon learned that Tim's mouth had no filter. When the professor overheard Tim tell Greg that her hairstyle reminded him of a frightened cat, she had dismissed him from class immediately. Greg had taken Tim a copy of his notes later that evening, and each semester had brought them closer.

Tim was a redhead who had never quite grown into his height. Though he was clumsy and forgetful at times, Tim was Greg's most loyal guy friend. Because Tim's fiancée was one of Melissa's best friends, the couples spent a lot of time together and often went on weekend double dates.

"Hey, Tim. What's up?" Greg asked as he leaned into the trunk of his car to grab his cleats and a water bottle.

Tim shook his head and sauntered over to where Greg stood by the car. "Nothing much. I'm pumped for this game. You ready to play?" he asked.

Greg laughed. "I think I'm as ready as I'll ever be for a friendly pick-up game of two-hand tag football."

"Oh, come on, man. We both know it's more than just a friendly game," Tim said, slapping Greg on the back.

"No. You *think* it's more than just a friendly game." Greg paused and slammed the trunk. "It really *is* just a friendly game, Tim."

"Whatever you say, big boy," Tim said as the two walked toward the other guys already huddling and stretching on the grassy field that would soon become a battleground of testosterone.

"Hey, Tim, Greg," Cooper said when the two men walked up. Cooper, a freshman at Covenant, was the newest member of their weekly football games. Though he was the youngest, he was over six feet tall and built like a wrestler.

"Hey, Cooper. How's it going?" Greg asked.

"It's great. Classes are done for the day. It's almost the weekend. December's just around the corner. I'm a happy man," Cooper said, grinning.

"That's great, Coop," Greg said.

"Wait! Today's the big day, right? Have you made your decision?" Cooper asked.

Greg shook his head. "It is the big day, but I still don't know what I'm going to tell Pastor Dyson. He told me I could call him as late as nine tonight." He paused, thinking. "I guess I'm kind of hoping God will just write the answers in the clouds this afternoon."

"I know what you mean. When I was choosing between colleges last year, I prayed for a neon sign. Never saw it. Not that I really expected to either," Cooper said.

Greg nodded. "I've asked for that one, too. I'm sure everyone thinks I'll take the job back home because it makes sense – my family's there, my wife wants to move back, my grandfather was a pastor there years ago…" Greg's voice trailed off as he watched the other guys toss the football a few yards away. "I just don't want to do the easy thing, you know?"

"I do, and I'm praying for you. I know you'll make the right decision," Cooper said.

"Thanks, Coop. For real, it means a lot," Greg said. "Now, who's ready for some football?"

*

Two hours later, Tim threw a game-winning Hail Mary pass to Greg in the corner of the end zone. When the ball slipped through his fingers, the other team celebrated at midfield before forming a line to congratulate Greg, Tim, and their teammates on a hard fought game.

Greg grabbed his water bottle and sat on the ground. He was in the middle of taking a long drink when Tim walked over. Tim looked down at Greg, his brow creased in concern. "Hey, man. Are you okay? You seemed a little out of it today?"

"Yeah, I'm all right. Just have a lot on my mind, I guess," Greg said. "Sorry I dropped that last pass. It was a beauty."

Tim shrugged. "No biggie. You win some. You lose some. You still thinking about the decision you have to make?"

Greg nodded. "I am. Just wish I knew what was right."

Tim squatted beside his friend. "Mind if I say something?"

"No, not at all," Greg said.

Tim grabbed a piece of grass and twisted it around his fingers. "I'm not known for giving good advice, so you can take this or leave it, but I can't help but think that if God doesn't tell you to go, maybe He wants you to stay. Because perhaps He's not finished with you yet."

Greg stared at his friend, stunned speechless. "Where'd you hear that?" he asked.

Tim shrugged. "Nowhere. I guess it just kind of came to me earlier when you were talking to Cooper. Sounds kind of smart, huh?" He grinned, clearly proud of himself.

Greg smiled and got to his feet. "It does. I've never thought about it that way before. Thanks, Tim."

"No problem," Tim said. "I think I might have to write that one down for future use. You leaving?"

Greg nodded. "Yeah. I've got some praying to do," he said, waving as he turned to go.

"See you later, man. Praying for you," Tim said.

Greg walked slowly to his car while his thoughts waged war against each other. He tossed his cleats into the back seat, climbed behind the wheel, and whispered a promise into the silence of the vehicle.

"Okay, God. If You don't tell me to go, I'm staying right here," Greg promised.

*

Greg stepped out of the shower and wrapped his towel around his waist. A glance at the digital clock on the bathroom counter told him Melissa wouldn't be home for another half hour. With the corner of the towel, Greg cleared a small circle in the foggy mirror and combed his hair. He slipped on the sweats he'd left strewn on the floor after his shower that morning and tossed the towel over the shower rod to dry.

Greg took his Bible from the nightstand and grabbed a red Gatorade from the refrigerator before settling into his favorite chair, a soft, brown recliner, in the sparsely decorated living room. To his left, an old floral couch sat beneath one of the room's windows. At Melissa's insistence, the old couch was kept covered with a sheet during the day to protect the already fading fabric from the sun's harsh rays. A picture of the kiss he and Melissa shared at their wedding ceremony hung framed on the wall opposite the couch. Below it, a small television sat atop a bar stool she bought last year at a rummage sale.

Greg set his Bible on his lap, studying the black leather cover, worn from years of use. The Bible had been a gift from his grandparents on the day of his high school graduation, the day he shared his call to the ministry with his family.

"Okay, God. I'm here. Show me something," he prayed aloud.

Greg pulled back the cover and read over the books listed in the table of contents. When he reached Revelation, the last book on the list, his eyes seemed drawn back to the Old Testament book of Jeremiah.

"Jeremiah? That's where You want me to start?" Greg whispered as he leafed through the thin pages and stopped at the book considered to be the second of the Major Prophets. "That's a pretty big book, God. Do You think You could narrow it down just a little bit?"

Greg chuckled, imagining how silly he would look if Melissa came home and saw him reclining in the chair, talking to an empty room. He shook his head, willing the thought away.

Greg sat silently, waiting for direction, as the seconds turned to minutes. Because he expected an audible answer, he was surprised when two numbers were impressed on his mind.

Chapter fourteen or nineteen.

"Okay, God. Two chapters? I can work with that," he thought as he turned to chapter fourteen.

A minute later, Greg finished reading the fourteenth chapter of Jeremiah and shook his head. "Hmm, that's good, God, but do you have anything else? I'm not really dealing with a drought or famine, or even the sword."

Greg flipped two pages to the right, the paper rustling with the movement. He placed his finger on the top of the page and traced down the text, stopping at the number nineteen. His mouth grew dry and his hands trembled when his eyes landed on the first seven words of the chapter: "This is what the Lord says: Go."

The Last Melon

Matthew 7:11 – If you, then, though you are evil, know how to give good gifts to your children, how much more will your Father in heaven give good gifts to those who ask Him!

  Lynsee guided her orange Volkswagen beetle up the dirt road before steering the car to the edge of the driveway and parking it beside her aunt's metal carport. Leaning over the center console, she grabbed the watermelon her grandma had asked her to pick up at the farmer's market, careful not to let the stem pick the seats of her car. She climbed out of the driver's seat and pushed the door closed. When she pressed the lock button on her key fob, the car beeped in response.

Slipping her keys in the pocket of her basketball shorts, Lynsee opened the gate in the chain link fence that surrounded her aunt's property and lugged the watermelon up the stone pathway to the back door of the trailer. She knocked on the glass door that separated the porch from the living room and took a step back. Her foot hit a small water bowl that belonged to her aunt's dog, causing the water to splash out of the blue plastic bowl and onto the wooden deck.

While she waited for someone to answer the door, Lynsee looked around the open-air porch and across the pool deck and backyard where she had spent many holiday afternoons. She smiled, remembering the games of freeze tag and hide-and-seek she had played with her cousins while her dad and uncles discussed football games over the grill.

The door opened, pulled inward by her aunt, and Lynsee stepped into the air-conditioned living room, which offered an escape from the sweltering June heat characteristic of South Carolina summers.

"Hi, Aunt Angie. Thank you," Lynsee said.

Aunt Angie was a short woman whose dark hair was shaped into a bowl cut. She hugged Lynsee tightly and planted a wet kiss on her cheek. "You're welcome, honey. It's so good to see you," Aunt Angie said.

Coal, the eight-pound toy poodle that belonged to Lynsee's youngest cousin, ran into the living room and stood on his hind legs begging for attention. Lynsee handed the watermelon to her aunt and bent down and picked up the energetic puppy, petting the dog's soft curly black fur in an attempt to calm him down.

"It's good to see you, too," Lynsee said as she moved her head side to side, dodging the small, pink poodle tongue.

"Coal, stop that. She doesn't want your kisses," Aunt Angie scolded, gently tapping the dog's head with her hand.

Lynsee laughed. "It's okay. He's just saying hi." Coal stuck his tongue out again, this time finding Lynsee's mouth.

"Well, if you get tired of him, you can put him in the crate," Aunt Angie said. She walked across the small living room, her socked feet silent on the hardwood floor, and placed the watermelon on the kitchen counter. "Pawpaw's in the back. I'll take him to the bathroom and bring him in here so y'all can visit."

"Okay. Do you need any help?" Lynsee asked.

"I've got it, sweetie. Just make yourself comfortable. If you want something to eat or drink, you know where it is," Aunt Angie said as she left the room.

Coal followed Lynsee into the kitchen, where she found a large knife and cut the watermelon into slices. After arranging several pieces on a serving platter, Lynsee sat down on the tan suede sofa in the living room and set Coal on her lap. A matching loveseat was pushed against the wall to her left, framed on either side by floor lamps. To her right, two large, rectangular windows were covered by thin, horizontal blinds, which filtered the harsh sunlight as it entered the room. Lynsee grabbed the remote control from the armrest and pointed it toward the large television that hung above the stone fireplace on the opposite side of the room. Family photographs lined the mantle and hung on the walls, an indication of the things considered most valuable in the house.

Lynsee heard the shuffle of feet across the linoleum kitchen floor and looked up to see her aunt assisting Pawpaw as he used a walker to help him move toward the living room. Once young and spry, Pawpaw's health had been rapidly deteriorating. In recent months, he had grown more stooped and battled constant chills. Thick glasses framed his kind eyes, and a horseshoe of gray and white hair circled his head.

Lynsee stood, pushing Coal off her lap, and moved to the other side of her grandfather, guiding his walker over the threshold that separated the kitchen and living room.

"Would you like to sit in your chair?" Aunt Angie asked her father.

Pawpaw nodded.

"Lynsee, honey, will you stand behind the chair and push it forward while I lower Dad into the chair?" Aunt Angie asked.

"Yes, ma'am, of course," Lynsee said and quickly moved around the big, dark green recliner.

When Pawpaw was positioned comfortably in his favorite chair, Aunt Angie waved Lynsee into the kitchen.

"I took him to the bathroom, so he should be okay until Meemaw gets back," she said.

Lynsee nodded. "Got it. And if he needs to go, I'll help him. No big deal."

"Meemaw's getting her hair done, but she should be back in a couple of hours. I'd think noon at the latest," Aunt Angie said. She grabbed her purse from the back of one of the kitchen chairs and slung it over her shoulder. "I'll be in the office at school, so if you need anything, call my cell phone, okay?"

"You got it, but I'm sure we'll be just fine," Lynsee said with a smile.

Aunt Angie hugged her again and planted another kiss on her cheek. "Thank you so much for coming over to watch Pawpaw. After he fell again over the weekend, Mom and I decided it would be best for someone to be with him at all times. We appreciate it more than you know."

"Really, I'm happy to help. These moments are fleeting, and I want to remember all of them," Lynsee said as she followed her aunt to the door.

Aunt Angie bent over Pawpaw and kissed the top of his head. "I'll see you in a little while, Dad. Lynsee's going to stay with you until Mom gets back. You be good for her, you hear?"

"I'll be good," Pawpaw said in his raspy, southern drawl.

"Will you lock the door behind me, honey?" Aunt Angie asked.

"Of course," Lynsee said as she rested her hand on the doorknob.

Coal ran toward Aunt Angie. "No, Coal. You're staying here with us," Lynsee said as she used her foot to block the dog's path to the door.

Aunt Angie slipped out the door, waving goodbye over her shoulder as she crossed the porch to her gold minivan. Lynsee locked the door and returned to her seat on the sofa. She looked over at her grandfather, noting the paleness of his skin and the wrinkles that added to the weariness on his face.

"Is there something you'd like to watch, Pawpaw?" Lynsee asked.

"I don't reckon it really matters to me," Pawpaw said. "Are there any game shows on?"

Lynsee picked up the remote and programmed the television to the guide channel. She watched the screen in silence as the shows scrolled up the screen, looking for the title of a game show to appear. Finally she saw the name of a show she recognized.

"How about *Family Feud*?" Lynsee asked, already changing the channel.

"That one would suit me just fine," Pawpaw said, pushing his hands further into the pockets of his fleece jacket.

"Would you like for me to get you a blanket?" Lynsee asked.

Pawpaw looked at her and smiled slightly. "I think a blanket might be real nice." He placed his hands on the armrests of the chair and started to push himself up. "But I can get it."

Lynsee stood quickly. "It's okay, Pawpaw. I'd love to get it. I'm already up." She watched her grandfather until he settled back into the chair and she was convinced that he wouldn't try to get up.

Lynsee pulled a red quilt from the bottom shelf of a nearby bookcase, keeping watch on her grandfather from the corner of her eye the entire time. She opened the blanket and spread it across her grandfather, tucking it between his body and the sides of the chair and underneath his chin. As she stood inches away from Pawpaw, Lynsee noticed that his hands and face were covered in minor scratches and bruises. *Those must have been from the fall he took this weekend,* she surmised.

"How's that?" Lynsee asked, stepping back to admire her handiwork.

Pawpaw smiled. "That feels real nice."

Lynsee settled back into the soft couch. Coal barked and tried unsuccessfully to jump up and join her. Lynsee bent over and set the small dog gingerly on the couch beside her, but Coal crawled onto her lap and curled up in a ball.

"That dog sure does like you," Pawpaw said.

Lynsee looked up to see her grandfather smiling at her, his head the only thing visible above the blanket cocooned around his body. "He seems to tolerate me at least," Lynsee said with a wink.

Pawpaw laughed. "You didn't have school this morning?" he asked.

"No, sir. I'm not taking summer classes this year," Lynsee said.

Pawpaw nodded. "Oh, that's right. It's summer," he mumbled.

When Pawpaw reverted his attention back to the television, Lynsee took the opportunity to stare at her grandfather, trying to memorize every detail of his face, each thin hair that stuck up on the top of his head.

"Don't you have a birthday soon?" Pawpaw asked. He turned to face Lynsee.

"It's in a couple months," Lynsee said, smiling despite the sadness she felt at her grandfather's growing confusion.

"A couple months," Pawpaw repeated softly. "What's your favorite birthday meal?"

Lynsee pursed her lips and drummed her fingers on her thighs as she considered the question. "I think that'd have to be my mom's chicken pot pie," she said. "And she usually makes mac and cheese, creamed corn, and green beans as the sides. It's *so* good."

"Is that right?" he asked, though it was more a statement than a question.

"What's your favorite meal?" Lynsee asked, pretty sure she already knew the answer.

Pawpaw didn't hesitate. "I reckon I could go for a steak and slice of watermelon just about any time."

Lynsee jumped up from the couch and ran to the kitchen. "I almost forgot. Meemaw asked me to bring a watermelon. Would you like a slice now?" she called to Pawpaw.

"I think that sounds wonderful," Pawpaw said. "I do love watermelon."

Lynsee grabbed two plates and two slices of watermelon and carried them into the den. She smiled, remembering how almost every holiday meal she'd ever shared with her dad's side of the family had included one of her grandfather's favorite foods.

Lynsee set one of the plates on the blanket in Pawpaw's lap. "Here you go. Maybe we could see about having a steak dinner sometime soon," Lynsee said.

Pawpaw nodded, his eyes focused on the juicy slice of watermelon before him. They ate in silence, and when Lynsee glanced over at her grandfather a few minutes later, he was asleep in the recliner with his head tilted back and his mouth open. The plate with the watermelon rind perched precariously on the blanket. Lynsee smiled and shook her head as she carried both plates to the kitchen, amazed at Pawpaw's ability to fall asleep so quickly. His quiet snores continued for the next hour as she watched the end of *Family Feud* and the beginning of *Let's Make a Deal*. Coal lay nestled in Lynsee's lap, his paws occasionally batting at the air as he chased after imaginary creatures in his dreams.

When she heard a key in the door behind her, Lynsee jumped, waking Coal from his sleep. Lynsee turned around to see her grandmother standing at the door. Part Cherokee, Meemaw's skin had a perpetual caramel bronze. Her short hair was white at the roots, hinting that the brown curls were not her natural color.

Meemaw was trying to stick her key in the lock and balance several grocery bags in her hands at the same time. Rushing to the door, Lynsee opened it and removed a few of the bags from her grandmother's arm.

"Hi, Meemaw. Let me help you with those," she said.

"Thank you, dear. I appreciate that," Meemaw said.

At the sound of his wife's voice, Pawpaw awoke from his nap and turned toward the door.

"Hi, Mom. Do you need some help?" Pawpaw asked, as he wiggled toward the edge of the chair.

"No. You stay put. Lynsee's helping me," Meemaw said as she stood beside the chair and used her free hand to pat her husband's arm. "We're going to set these things on the kitchen table. We'll be right back."

While Lynsee followed Meemaw to the kitchen, she kept an eye on her grandfather. Once an able-bodied farmer and handy man, now even the simplest acts caused him to lose his balance and fall. The transformation was striking.

Meemaw set the grocery bags on the kitchen table and turned to Lynsee. "Thank you so much for watching Pawpaw today, dear. It was nice to be able to get out of the house for a little while," Meemaw said.

"I was glad to, Meemaw. Really. We had a good time and got to talk about a lot of things," Lynsee said. She bent over to hug her grandmother, catching a whiff of the beauty salon chemicals still lingering in her grandmother's hair. "Your hair looks really good, by the way."

Meemaw laughed. "I'm not sure it looks good, but it at least looks better than it did."

"Can I help you put the groceries away?" Lynsee asked, eyeing the bags spread across the table.

"No, it's okay. I can handle it," Meemaw said.

Lynsee hesitated. "Are you sure? I don't mind."

Meemaw shook her head and, placing a hand on Lynsee's back, guided her toward the living room. "You've already done enough. Run along and enjoy your day."

Lynsee smiled. "Well, if you're sure…"

"I'm sure. There aren't that many groceries anyway, and one of the kids should be home soon if I need help," Meemaw said as she led the way back to the living room.

Meemaw leaned in for another hug, and Lynsee wrapped her arms around her grandmother's small frame before leaning over the chair to tell her grandfather goodbye as well. "I'll see you later. Okay, Pawpaw?"

Pawpaw smiled and pulled his arms out from under the blanket. He pulled Lynsee close. "Okay. I love you," he whispered in her ear.

Lynsee smiled. She couldn't remember a single time her grandfather had forgotten to tell her he loved her, and now, despite his declining health and forgetful tendencies, he didn't miss the opportunity to remind her of his love.

"I love you, too, Pawpaw," she said as she stood and turned toward the door.

*

A week later, Lynsee stuck her key in the lock of the sunroom door and turned the handle as the hot summer sun beat down on her shoulders. She stepped inside her house and dropped her beach towel and lifeguard duffle bag on the ground, pushing the sliding glass door closed behind her.

The house was surprisingly quiet for a summer afternoon. She slipped her feet out of her flip-flops and padded across the room to the adjoining kitchen. On the table near the doorway Lynsee found a note and immediately recognized her mother's handwriting.

> *Pawpaw fell again. Dad and I are at Aunt Angie's with Meemaw and his sisters. Your brothers are playing ultimate Frisbee. Get dinner with them when they get back. Text me when you get this. We'll call you if you need to come, otherwise, we'll see you later tonight.*
>
> *Mom*

Lynsee pulled one of the wooden kitchen chairs away from the table and sat down, letting the reality of the situation sink in. Just days ago she had been visiting with her grandfather, and it had been less than a week since his last accident. She reread the note, searching for any hidden message or sense of urgency she might have missed. When she didn't see one, she grabbed her cell phone out of the duffel bag at her feet and texted her mom.

*

Several hours later, Lynsee was watching a movie on the brown playroom sofa when she heard the sunroom door slide open. At the sound, her brothers, Carter and Bryson, paused their online video games and looked toward the door. At twenty, Carter was two years younger than Lynsee but stood half a foot taller. His wavy brown hair was highlighted from the hours spent in the sun while he volunteered at a youth camp earlier in the summer. Bryson was the baby of the family and had just turned fifteen. He kept his blond hair short and out of the way of his clear blue eyes.

Lynsee turned her attention from her brothers to her parents, Russell and Sherri, who had just stepped into the room. Her mom looked tired. Her brown hair hung limply at her shoulders, and the crow's feet around her eyes were more pronounced than usual. Even her dad, who was the perpetual jokester, didn't crack a smile with his hello. His mouth was set in a line, and dark circles had formed under his eyes.

Lynsee sat up on the sofa, making room for her parents to sit down. Her father was the first to speak.

"Pawpaw fell again this afternoon," he began, running a hand through his short, dark brown hair. "Angela and Meemaw were both home, but they didn't hear him calling for help to go to the bathroom, so he decided to go on his own. He didn't make it more than a few steps before he fell in the living room, slamming his head onto the hardwood floor."

"He wasn't able to put his hands out to catch himself?" Lynsee asked.

Her mother shook her head. "It doesn't appear that he did. Of course, no one was there to see it. When Angela and Meemaw heard a loud thump, they came running into the room and found Pawpaw lying on the floor."

"Did they take him to the doctor?" Carter asked. He leaned forward and set his laptop on a nearby computer desk, focusing his attention solely on his parents. Lynsee could sense his apprehension from the furrows in his brow.

Her father shook his head slowly. "No. He refused to go see a doctor. He's tired of taking countless medications around the clock and of having to travel back and forth to doctor's appointments every few days."

"So, that means..." Lynsee's voice trailed off but her eyes remained on the hunched figure of her father.

He nodded and brought a fist to his mouth. Lynsee looked at her mother, who placed an arm around her husband's back. After what seemed like hours, it was her mother who said the words Lynsee couldn't bring herself to voice aloud. "The blow to his head was pretty bad. It left severe bruising," she paused before continuing, "but it's what we can't see that is the problem. There's probably internal bleeding and swelling of the brain."

"So we just wait?" Bryson asked. "Like, for him to die?"

Lynsee stood and walked over to where he sat alone on the floor. Sitting down beside him, she wrapped her arms protectively around her littlest brother's shoulders.

"Angela called his doctor and explained the situation. We've hired a hospice worker to be around at all times. She'll regulate his pain medication and keep him as comfortable as possible," her father said.

Lynsee took a deep breath before asking her next question. "Can we see him?"

Her mother nodded. "Yes, of course. I think it would be best if we wait a day or two until things get settled, but Angela will call if things take a turn for the worst and we need to rush over."

*

"Lynsee. Sweetheart, wake up."

Lynsee felt a hand on her shoulder, gently shaking her awake. She caught a glimpse of the clock as she rolled over in bed. 4:02. Despite the darkness of the room, Lynsee was able to make out the outline of her mother's face staring down at her.

"What is it, Mom? What's wrong?" Even as the words left her lips, Lynsee's heart sank. She could only think of one reason for an early morning wake-up call: her grandfather.

"It's Pawpaw. We don't think he has much longer," her mother said. "Your father is waking up the boys. We need to leave now."

Lynsee nodded and scrambled out of bed. "Do I have time to put some clothes on?"

Her mother stopped in the doorway, her body silhouetted by the light from the hallway. She nodded, "Yes, but be quick. We'll leave in five minutes."

Lynsee bumped into her nightstand and stubbed her toe on her dresser as she searched her drawers for a pair of sweatpants. Finding a pair thrown over the side of her dirty clothes hamper, she slipped them on and pulled her hair out of her face with a rubber band from her bathroom counter.

She found her brothers waiting for her on the sunroom couch. They were silent, a fact she wasn't sure should be attributed to the time of day or the reason they were all awake.

"You ready?" Carter asked as he stood.

Lynsee nodded. "But don't we need to wait for Mom and Dad?"

The guys moved toward the door. "They're waiting in the car," Bryson said, pointing out the glass door to the light blue minivan sitting in the driveway with its lights on. He held the door open for Lynsee and slid it shut behind her.

*

The drive to Aunt Angie's trailer was quiet, making the five-minute trip seem to take hours. Lynsee tried to prepare herself for the worst, though she wasn't sure what that would look like. It was hard to imagine her grandfather as anything other than the strong, happy gentleman she'd always known him to be.

After her dad pulled the car off the dirt driveway and parked it alongside her cousin's truck, he turned around to Lynsee and her brothers. "I don't know exactly what we're going to find when we go in there. All Angela told me is that the hospice nurse said it wouldn't be long now. If you want to see him, you'll be allowed to, but if you would rather wait in the living room, everyone will understand."

Lynsee climbed out of the back seat after her brothers and grabbed her mom's arm as they followed the guys toward the house.

"You okay?" her mom asked.

Lynsee nodded, her words sticking in her throat.

Since the back door was unlocked, her dad pushed it open and let his family file through. The only light in the room came from a lamp by the couch, which cast shadows across the floor. Lynsee saw her cousins asleep on the couch and pointed out their presence to the rest of her family, who tiptoed quietly out of the room and through the kitchen toward the back of the house.

Aunt Angie intercepted the group in the hallway. "The medication makes him drowsy so he's dozing, but y'all go on in," she whispered. "Meemaw's in there."

Lynsee watched her dad push the bedroom door open and peer through the crack. He stepped closer to his family and said, "There's not much room, so let's just send two or three people in at a time. Who wants to go first?"

Lynsee looked at her brothers, who both shook their heads. "I will," she said softly.

"Sherri, why don't you go with her," Lynsee's father said.

Lynsee pushed the bedroom door open wide enough for her mom to follow her through before letting it swing closed behind them. Upon entering the bedroom, Lynsee was encompassed by the almost stifling warmth of the room, which she tried to ignore. She figured that since Pawpaw was always cold, the temperature had been adjusted to make him comfortable.

The room was dark except for the glow of a single nightlight, which illuminated the room enough for Lynsee to detect the shape of her grandmother sitting in a chair beside the bed where Pawpaw lay. She crossed the room silently, bending over to hug her grandmother before turning her attention to her grandfather.

Lynsee stared down at her grandfather's motionless body. The slight rise and fall of his chest served as the only indication that he was still breathing.

Lynsee heard Meemaw's voice from behind her and glanced over her shoulder to see her mother holding her grandma's hand. "They say he can hear you," Meemaw said, her voice cracking either from weariness or the strain of emotion.

Lynsee bent down beside her grandfather's bed and took one of his cold hands in her own. She laid her head beside his on the pillow and positioned her mouth near his ear.

"Hey, Pawpaw. I don't know if you can hear me, but I want you to know that I'm praying for you. So many people are." She paused, fighting back tears. "I love you."

Lynsee stood and leaned over to kiss her grandfather's wrinkled forehead. As she pulled away, Pawpaw's eyes fluttered open, and in his familiar, raspy voice he uttered one simple phrase. "I love you."

*

Lynsee took a deep breath and looked out over the small crowd that had gathered in the funeral home chapel to honor the memory of her grandfather. From the tan walls to the dark green carpet, the interior of the building was simply decorated in earthy tones. Two rows of wooden pews spread out in front of her, and from her place behind the large podium that took up much of the space on the small stage, Lynsee could see each guest clearly. Her eyes rested on her grandmother, who was seated between two of her children in the front row, before returning to the paper in front of her. She started reading.

"While I don't know that any one word could possibly sum up everything my grandfather was, I have found what I believe to be the best fit for a one-word description of Pawpaw. That word is love.

"Pawpaw loved many people and many things. Nothing was greater than his love for the Lord, and it is because of this love that I have no doubt he is in the presence of our Father even now.

"Just last week, I was spending some one-on-one time with Pawpaw, and I was reminded of his love for food, specifically steak and watermelon."

Suppressed laughter rose from the front row where Lynsee's family sat. She couldn't help but smile and gather strength from their support.

"And none of us," Lynsee glanced up at the familiar faces of her grandmother, her parents, and her aunts and uncles and cousins, "would dream of doubting Pawpaw's love for his wife.

"Early that Monday morning was the last time I spoke with my grandfather. Our conversation was incredibly short. As I leaned over to give him a hug, I whispered, 'I love you' in his ear, and I will forever be grateful to my heavenly Father that Pawpaw's last words to me this side of heaven were none other than that simple, heartfelt phrase in return.

"If he was here, I think my grandfather would agree that life is short and time is precious. I think he would encourage us to hug those we love, laugh at life, and never miss a chance to say, 'I love you.' Because, as 1 Corinthians 13:8 so perfectly says, 'Love never fails.'"

Lynsee folded her notes and moved out from behind the podium. The pastor offered her his hand as she carefully descended the stage. She smiled her thanks before slipping past several family members and taking her seat on the pew beside them.

Before she knew it, the pianist played the first notes of the final hymn, and Lynsee stood and followed the other members of her family down the center aisle and out the back of the small chapel. She climbed into the black limousine that was waiting outside and sat on one of the leather seats across from her grandmother.

As the limo pulled away from the curb, Aunt Angie turned to Meemaw. "That was a beautiful service, Mom. I know Dad would've been proud."

Meemaw smiled and nodded. "It sure was." She looked at Lynsee. "You did a wonderful job. I know it wasn't easy, but your words meant the world to me. Thank you." She reached across the limo and squeezed her hand.

"You're welcome, Meemaw. Pawpaw was a special man. I just hope everyone else was able to see that today," Lynsee said. She looked past her grandmother and out the tinted window of the limousine. "I love how everyone pulls over to the side of the road when they see a funeral procession. Is it like that everywhere?"

Her dad, who was sitting next to her, shook his head. "It's mainly a small town thing, a taste of Southern hospitality."

"I like that," Lynsee said. "Oh my gosh. Y'all, look!"

Removing her hand from her grandmother's grip, Lynsee pointed at something outside one of the tinted windows. Her family members turned their heads, craning to see what had grabbed her attention.

Two of the cars in the police escort had pulled to the side of the road, blocking off the final intersection between the funeral home and the cemetery so the entire processional could pass through together. However that was not what Lynsee had noticed.

"Well, what do you know." Meemaw was the first to speak, her soft words evidence of the wonder she felt.

For there, spread throughout the intersection and along the side of the road, were shattered and whole watermelons that looked like they'd fallen from the back of a truck.

Lynsee watched a tear trickle down her grandmother's face. "No one around town even grows watermelons," Meemaw whispered, giving voice to the thought that had already settled in Lynsee's mind. "What are the odds we'd see some right here, right now?" she finished, her voice trailing off.

Lynsee looked at the faces surrounding her and marveled at the goodness of God. *You knew we needed a reason to believe, and You cared enough to supply that reason. Thanks. I'll never look at a watermelon the same way again.*

The Midnight Visitor

Exodus 23:20 – "Behold, I send an angel before you to guard you on the way and to bring you to the place that I have prepared."

    Jeremy Corbin picked up his glass and took a sip of the iced tea before returning the cup to the table. His gaze never left the beautiful woman sitting across from him. Though he and Michelle had only been dating for three months, Jeremy couldn't imagine life without her. *Hopefully I won't have to after tonight. If she's really the woman I think she is, she'll understand*

and won't hold it against me. Or will she? His thoughts warred against each other.

His friends often poked fun at him, asking how he'd managed to catch a girl like Michelle, and if he was being honest, he had to agree with them. At a stocky five-foot-eight and in his mid-thirties, Jeremy lacked most of the qualities considered attractive and felt he was certainly past his prime.

Michelle, on the other hand, was graceful and gentle. At thirty-two, she was as fit as she'd been during her volleyball days in high school. Michelle was tall and thin, with silky brown hair that hung down past her shoulders. She had no need for makeup because her green eyes were accented by her olive complexion.

Michelle took another bite of her spaghetti and looked up from her plate to see Jeremy staring at her.

"What're you looking at, Jer?" Michelle asked through a mouthful of pasta. She wiped her mouth with a napkin and checked the front of her shirt for red stains then returned her gaze to Jeremy. "Do I have sauce all over my face?"

"Hello? Earth to Jeremy?" she asked, waving her hand in front of his face.

Jeremy shook his head quickly and smiled sheepishly. "Sorry, Michelle. No, you look beautiful as always."

Michelle smiled and cocked her head. "Thanks, hon. You make me feel like it, but is something the matter? You seem a little spacey tonight."

"No, everything's great. I'm in this fancy Italian restaurant having dinner with the girl of my dreams." Jeremy held his hands up at his sides. "What more could I possibly ask for?"

"Michelle laughed. "Now you're just laying it on thick. You must want something."

"The only thing I want is sitting across from me right now," Jeremy said with a wink.

Michelle blushed and bit her lip. She dabbed the corners of her mouth with her napkin before setting it on the table and leaning back in her chair.

"You can't be finished," Jeremy said, eyeing his girlfriend's half-eaten plate of pasta.

Michelle placed her hands on her flat stomach and stuck her bottom lip out. "I'm so full, but it was so good." She leaned to her right and looked around the candle centerpiece at Jeremy's plate. "Besides, you didn't finish your lasagna either."

"I'm just picking on you," Jeremy said, raising his hand to summon the young waiter who had been serving the couple. "We're ready for the check, please," Jeremy said. "And could we also get two boxes for the leftovers?"

The boy nodded and hurried away from the table, his curly brown hair bouncing as he weaved through the maze of tables in the dining room. He returned moments later carrying a tray that held two Styrofoam boxes and the small black checkbook.

"Here you are, sir," the waiter said as he placed the boxes on the table and handed Jeremy the bill. Turning to Michelle, the waiter asked, "May I take care of your leftovers, ma'am?"

Michelle's eyebrows shot up in surprise. She looked to Jeremy, who shrugged as he calculated the tip on his phone and stuck a wad of cash in the waiter's book.

"Oh, no, thank you," Michelle stammered. "I can take care of it."

Jeremy held the book out to the waiter. "Here you go, sir. It's all yours. Thank you very much for your wonderful service tonight."

The boy nodded, bowing slightly to Jeremy and Michelle. "Thank you. Have a wonderful evening," he said as he backed away from the table.

Jeremy dumped his lasagna into one of the boxes before he stood and carried the other box to Michelle's side of the table.

"May I take care of your leftovers for you?" Jeremy asked. As he leaned over her plate of food and reached for her utensils, a grin spread across his face.

Michelle jabbed him playfully in the ribs. "Stop that. I wasn't expecting him to ask, and I didn't know what to say." She laughed. "But yes, please do. There's no one else I'd rather have taking care of me," she said, kissing him quickly on the cheek.

*

Half an hour later, Michelle was snuggled up next to Jeremy on the worn leather couch in his den. The focal point of the room was the large flat screen television that hung on the wall opposite the couch. With football posters plastered on the wood-paneled walls for decoration, brown shag carpet on the floor, and a mini-fridge tucked in the corner, the room was the epitome of a man cave.

At Michelle's request, Jeremy had agreed to watch a Hallmark Christmas movie. A bowl of popcorn sat untouched on a small coffee table in the middle of the room. Condensation formed water droplets that slid down two Coke cans and landed on paperboard coasters Jeremy had pilfered from a local restaurant.

When a commercial interrupted the movie, Michelle grabbed the remote and muted the television. Michelle sat up and crossed her legs in front of her. Taking Jeremy's face in her hands, she looked into his eyes. "I know something's bothering you," she said. "You've been different all night. Quiet."

Jeremy dropped his gaze to his lap. He took a deep breath as he folded Michelle's thin hands into his own, not daring to look into the eyes of the woman he loved so much. When they started dating, he hadn't known he would fall so hard or so fast.

"You can talk to me about anything. Please tell me what's wrong," Michelle whispered, craning her neck to meet his gaze.

Tears welled up in Jeremy's eyes, but he blinked them back, willing himself to regain his composure. His voice cracked when he spoke. "Michelle, there's something I have to tell you," he began, carefully choosing his next words. "I love you, and I cannot imagine life without you. I love your smile. I love the way your hand fits perfectly in mine. I love the way you love life and the way you make me love life."

Michelle smiled and bit her lip. Though the only light in the room came from the television, Jeremy noticed that Michelle's cheeks were flushed.

"But?" she prodded.

"But I can't have kids," Jeremy blurted out.

Michelle's forehead knit together in confusion. "You can't have kids? That's what has been bothering you all night?"

Jeremy nodded, waiting for her to say something.

"I'm not sure I understand," she said. Her voice drifted off, but her eyes remained on Jeremy.

"I've met a lot of girls in my lifetime," Jeremy said. "But none of them have made me feel like you do. I want a future with you, but before I can ask you for one with me, I need you to know that I can't give you kids. I had testicular cancer when I was twenty-nine. The doctors told me having children is just not possible."

Realization dawned in Michelle's eyes. "And you think kids are a deal breaker for me? Because of what I told you last weekend when we saw that set of twins playing in the park downtown?"

Jeremy nodded and quickly wiped away a tear that was sliding down his face.

Michelle leaned in and kissed his cheek. "Well that's where you're wrong, Jeremy." She paused and combed her fingers through his hair. "I haven't fallen in love with the kids that you could or couldn't give me. I've fallen in love with you."

*

Michelle Corbin stood at the counter, chopping carrots and potatoes and dropping them into the large stew pot. The radio was tuned to her favorite country music station, and she hummed along to the popular Tim McGraw song.

Jeremy hung up the phone in the den and watched his wife, the way her hips swayed to the music and her long brown ponytail bobbed with each movement. He walked into the kitchen, his socked feet silent on the linoleum floor. As he pulled a chair out from under the kitchen table, its legs scraped across the floor, causing Michelle to turn around.

"Oh, you scared me!" she exclaimed.

"Sorry, honey. I didn't mean to," he said as he placed his elbows on the table and let his head fall into his hands.

Michelle studied her husband for a minute before rinsing and drying her hands. She crossed the kitchen and leaned over his shoulders from behind, wrapping her arms around his neck.

"That was your mom, right? Tell me what she said." Michelle's words were more statements than questions. She sat down in the chair beside Jeremy and placed a hand on his knee, waiting for him to speak.

"Her cancer's back," he finally said.

Jeremy watched Michelle's expression change from one of open-mouthed surprise to teary devastation.

Michelle sniffed and choked back a sob. "The same kind? It's skin cancer again?" she asked.

Jeremy nodded. Before he could say anything, Michelle jumped in with more questions. "But they treated it before, and they were successful, so they can do it again, right?"

Jeremy pressed his lips together and closed his eyes as he massaged his temples with his fingers. He slowly shook his head. "It doesn't look like it. You have to remember, that was over thirty years ago. Mom was a lot younger then."

"But she's not that old now."

"Honey, she's eighty-five," Jeremy said gently.

Michelle frowned and waved her hand in the air, dismissing the fact. "But she doesn't *act* like an eighty-something-year-old. She's been walking three miles every day for the twelve years we've been together. She's taken care of herself since your dad died forty-five years ago. She cooks, cleans, and pays the bills. She even eats a chewy Flintstone vitamin every morning and has Rascal Flatts on her iPod, for heaven's sake!" she finished.

"Shh, honey. It's not worth getting so worked up over," Jeremy said as he grabbed her hands from making circles in midair and held them between his own.

"Of course it is, Jeremy. She could die," Michelle said, tears flowing down her face.

Jeremy opened his arms and let Michelle fall into him. She laid her head on his chest, her slender body shaking with her sobs. Jeremy dried his eyes on the shoulder of his t-shirt and buried his face in her hair. He rubbed small, slow circles on her back, and eventually, she stopped crying.

When Michelle pulled back, her eyes were red and watery, and her nose was running. Jeremy grabbed a napkin from the counter and held it out to his wife. She dried her eyes and blew her nose. Taking a deep breath, she said, "I'm sorry. I should be the one consoling you. She's your mother, after all."

Jeremy smiled and tucked a stray piece of hair behind Michelle's ear. "It's okay, sweetheart. You love her, too. Heck, your whole family loves her. Remember when your dad invited her to his birthday dinner last year?"

Michelle laughed, her voice hoarse from crying. "I do. We walked in, and you did a double take. When you saw your mom setting the table, you thought we were at the wrong house."

Jeremy grinned. "That's just how she is, you know? You can't help but love her."

Michelle nodded then grew solemn. "Jeremy, I'm sorry Beth's cancer is back. Can you tell me what exactly she found out from the doctor? I promise I won't cry like that again."

"There isn't really much to tell," Jeremy said, letting his hands rest on his wife's shoulders. "Since the doctor first found the cancer when she was fifty, he's been checking her frequently. You knew that."

Michelle nodded. "I did," she whispered.

Jeremy took a deep breath before continuing. "Well, when she went two weeks ago for a regular check-up, the doctor found a patch of skin that concerned him. The biopsy came back positive. Apparently, the cancer has already spread to other parts of her body." Jeremy shrugged. "The doctor says he can't get it all."

Michelle frowned. Her pinched expression told Jeremy her feelings were hurt. "You knew all this, and you didn't tell me?" she asked.

He quickly shook his head. "No. She called me last week and told me she had an appointment scheduled for two days ago. I didn't think anything of it because she usually keeps me up to date on everything that's going on." He paused before continuing. "She called just now to tell me the results of the biopsy."

"So there's nothing that can be done? No chemo or anything?"

"Mom doesn't want to. She told me she's lived a good life and is ready to stop fighting."

"Will she stay at home then? Does she need to come here?" Michelle asked. "You know I'd love to have your mother live with us."

Jeremy smiled at his wife's compassion and love for his mother. "We haven't discussed it yet. Mom's still feeling pretty good right now, but the doctor said that could change quickly. I thought maybe we could have her over for dinner tomorrow night? We could discuss things then?"

"Of course," Michelle said. "You know she's always welcome in our home."

*

The drive home from the cemetery was quiet. Jeremy glanced at his wife in the passenger seat, her face turned away from him as she stared out the window. He reached for her hand, offering it a gentle squeeze.

Michelle squeezed back and looked at Jeremy. His heart broke when he saw her tear-stained cheeks and the smudges of mascara under her eyes.

"You're awfully quiet. Are you okay, sweetheart?" he asked.

Michelle nodded. "I just keep thinking about the service. I know Memorial Baptist Church isn't large, but the building was packed with all different kinds of people."

Jeremy nodded but kept his eyes on the road.

"I mean, there were young people and old people, white people and black people. We've been married for what, almost ten years? I knew I hadn't met all of Beth's friends, but I certainly thought I knew most of them. Well, at least until today," she added.

Jeremy chuckled. "I know what you mean. I always knew Mom was special, but I had no idea she had touched so many lives," his voice drifted off as he looked over his shoulder and changed lanes. Then he continued, "Growing up, I was bad about making judgments about other people. I can't count the number of times she waved a finger in my face and said 'You haven't walked in their shoes.' That's just how she was, you know? Assuming the best about everyone all the time."

"Today was certainly a testament to that," Michelle said.

Jeremy drove the remaining five minutes to their house in silence, letting Michelle's words sink in. He parked the car in the driveway and hustled around the hood to open the door for his wife.

"Thanks, honey," Michelle said as she climbed out and smoothed the front of her short, black dress. She grabbed her purse from the floorboard and slung it over her shoulder before walking toward the front door.

Jeremy watched as Michelle climbed the three steps to the front porch, inserted her key in the lock, and slipped through the glass door. He closed the passenger door and leaned against the car, grateful for a moment alone with his thoughts. He tipped his head back and studied the clouds that dotted the otherwise clear blue sky.

"Miss you already, Mom," he whispered, before locking the door and walking up the driveway.

The house was eerily quiet when he stepped inside. The screen door banged shut behind him, the sound echoing through the small foyer. Jeremy left his shoes by the door and loosened his tie as he walked down the hallway toward the master bedroom. He pushed the door open, expecting to find his wife changing out of her dress, but the room was empty.

"Michelle?" Jeremy called softly, not wanting to startle her.

When he heard nothing, Jeremy checked the closet and bathroom, but Michelle was in neither. Panicked, he rushed back to the hallway, calling louder. "Michelle? Michelle where are you?"

"I'm in here." Michelle's voice was soft and muffled.

Jeremy moved toward the sound. "Where, honey?" he asked.

"I'm right here," Michelle said, her voice strained. She stuck her hand through the doorway of the small storage room that was adjoined to their bedroom and waved. When she didn't step into the hallway, Jeremy walked toward the door and pushed his way inside.

The room was the size of a large walk-in closet. When they bought the house, the area was part of the master bedroom. Michelle had felt like the extra space made the room seem too large and less intimate, so Jeremy had constructed a wall of separation. At the time, they had jokingly referred to the room as the nursery, but the reality was that such a room would never be needed for their family. Instead, the room was filled with a miscellaneous collection of junk: old furniture, seasonal clothes, and unwanted Christmas gifts.

Michelle was standing by the only window in the room, which overlooked the small garden in their backyard. Jeremy walked over and stood behind his wife, wrapping his arms around her tiny waist. He rested his head on her shoulder and whispered into her ear. "What's wrong, honey?"

Michelle hiccupped and breathed deeply before turning to face Jeremy. "I want to have kids," she said.

Jeremy dropped his hands to his side and stepped backward. "What? We can't do that. *I* can't do that. You knew that, Michelle. I told you that."

Tears fell from Michelle's eyes so quickly that she no longer tried to wipe them away. "I know, but that was a long time ago. It's been more than a decade since you had the cancer," she paused, her breath coming in ragged gasps. "There have been so many medical advances since then. Maybe there's hope?"

Jeremy's throat felt like it was closing in on itself. He leaned against the doorframe for support. After regaining his composure he met his wife's gaze. "You've never mentioned kids before. What is this really about, Michelle?"

"Your mother," she whispered.

Jeremy dropped his arms and took a step closer to his wife. "Mom? What does this have to do with Mom?" he asked, placing his hands on her arms.

Michelle sighed. "When I was visiting her in the nursing home a few weeks ago, we got to talking about her life. We talked about her husband and about how she could never bring herself to marry anyone else because she couldn't imagine life with anyone but him. We talked about you and your older siblings, how y'all were the delight of her life. She told me about her nine brothers and sisters and what it was like growing up in a big family," Michelle paused to catch her breath. "And we talked about things she would've changed if she could."

Jeremy swallowed past the lump that had formed in his throat. "And?" he whispered.

"And her only regret was that, unlike all her siblings, she never had any grandchildren," Michelle said.

Jeremy clenched his fists and gritted his teeth. He closed his eyes and sank to his knees as he held his head in his hands. *After everything my mother did for me, I couldn't give her the one thing she wanted*, Jeremy thought in desperation.

Michelle knelt down beside him and took his hands in her own. When he looked up, her eyes were dry, and she was smiling. "I know what you're thinking," she said. "You feel guilty because you couldn't give her a grandchild."

Jeremy nodded, refusing to meet his wife's gaze. She lifted his chin with one of her hands and held it there until he looked at her.

"But that's not what she would've wanted. Jeremy, your brother or sister could have had kids if they'd wanted them, but they didn't. And your mom didn't resent them for it, just like she never would've dreamed of resenting you for your infertility. It didn't change her love for you, it couldn't have. She had a good life, and she knew it," Michelle said.

After several minutes, Jeremy spoke. "She would've been a wonderful grandmother."

Michelle leaned in and kissed him on the lips. When she pulled back, she was grinning. "Who says she can't be now?"

*

Jeremy and Michelle were alone in the waiting room at the fertility clinic. The room was plain. The walls were painted light blue and several paintings of lighthouses were spaced around the room. A single row of chairs lined the walls of the small waiting area. One wall of the waiting room was constructed entirely of windows, leaving privacy a thing to be imagined. Pregnancy magazines were stacked on top of the small wooden tables that were spread throughout the room.

Jeremy's hands were folded in his lap, and his knee bounced nervously. Michelle reached over and placed a hand on his leg. He held still and looked at her, offering the saddest puppy dog eyes he could muster.

"Stop that," Michelle said with a laugh. "And stop the bouncing, too. You're making me nervous."

"*I'm* making *you* nervous?" Jeremy asked, pointing from himself to his wife. "I don't think so."

Michelle nodded, a small smile formed on her lips.

Jeremy turned in his chair to look at her. "Are you doing okay? Really?" he asked.

"I am. I'm just ready to hear what the doctor has to say," Michelle said, her eyes wide in anticipation.

"Just don't get your hopes up. You know how small our chances are," Jeremy reminded her.

"So, you're telling me there's a chance." Michelle giggled as she repeated the line from *Dumb and Dumber*, the first movie they'd seen as a couple.

Jeremy laughed in spite of himself, but regained his composure quickly. "I mean it, honey. I know how strongly you feel about this, but there's the possibility that it's just not meant to be."

"I know, but it's hard not to hope," Michelle confessed. "Especially after you agreed to harvesting the eggs."

"Yes, but remember, there were only two considered viable. Add those odds to the fact that

I only had two sperm, and well, our chances are looking pretty slim," Jeremy said.

Michelle opened her mouth to answer when a high-pitched female voice said. "Mr. and Mrs. Corbin? The doctor will see you now."

Jeremy grabbed Michelle's hand and led her across the room to where the petite nurse, whose silver nametag read 'Felicia,' waited in the doorway. Felicia sported a blond pixie haircut, and her blue eyes matched the color of the waiting room walls.

"If you'll come with me, Dr. Arya is waiting for you," Felicia said as she led the couple down a series of winding hallways. She stopped in front of an open door about halfway down the final hallway and motioned for the couple to step inside.

As promised, Dr. Arya was already in the room. He sat on a rolling stool at a small desk in the corner of the room, his back turned to the couple. Jeremy cleared his throat, but the doctor didn't seem to notice. Failing to get the doctor's attention, Jeremy shrugged and led Michelle to the cushioned chairs situated on the opposite side of the doorway.

The room was small and contained minimal furniture. Aside from the chairs and desk, there was a small sink and an examination table. Posters of reproductive organs and charts detailing the trimesters of pregnancy hung on the white walls.

The couple held hands and stared at the back of the doctor's white coat. After a few minutes, Dr. Arya turned suddenly, causing Michelle to jump.

"How long have you been sitting there? You should have said something," the old doctor said, his voice tinged with a mild Indian accent. "I didn't hear you come in."

Jeremy looked at Michelle and raised his eyebrows in amusement.

Dr. Arya was in his late seventies and had been practicing medicine for more than half his life. He had come to the United States as a teenager. The doctor was balding, but what little hair he had left was white. His face was wrinkled with age and his thick glasses magnified his eyeballs, causing the pupils to appear double their actual size.

"Sorry, Doctor. You looked busy. We didn't want to interrupt you," Jeremy said.

Dr. Arya nodded once. "Ah, yes, I see." He held the couple's file in his hand. The folder was thick with test results, prescriptions, and notes from operations. "I must tell you that I've never seen a case quite like yours," the doctor began. "The odds of reproduction – from both of you – were the smallest I have seen in my thirty-nine years of practicing."

Jeremy's shoulders fell as the heaviness of the doctor's words set in. He glanced at his wife and felt a sting of pain at her smile that spoke of her unwavering optimism. He returned his attention to the doctor.

"Which is why, when I received your results, I had to read them twice. Just one fertilized egg would've been considered a success, but both eggs being fertilized? Well, it's extraordinary!"

Jeremy's head swam. *Am I hearing him right? Did he just say what I think he said? Both eggs were fertilized? My wife is carrying twins?* Jeremy tried to slow his racing thoughts. His wife's voice broke him out of his reverie.

"Are you saying I'm pregnant?" Michelle asked, her voice cracking.

Dr. Arya nodded. "I'm saying you're pregnant... with twins."

*

Jeremy rolled out of bed and grabbed a t-shirt from the back of the rocking chair beside the bed. After he slipped it over his head, he glanced at the clock. 3:12.

The twins have been asleep for four hours. This must be what heaven feels like, he thought.

Michelle was curled up in a ball in the middle of the bed. Jeremy stumbled toward the door of the dark bedroom. He needed to use the bathroom, but he refrained from using the master bath for fear of waking his sleeping wife. Jeremy stepped into the hallway, pulling the bedroom door closed behind him.

Jeremy padded down the hallway toward the guest bathroom but stopped abruptly in front of the storage room that had been converted into the twins' nursery. Under the crack at the bottom of the door, he saw a gold light, like from a candle or kerosene lamp, reflecting off the dark brown, varnished wood floor. He hesitated, thinking, *We don't even keep a lamp in the twins' room. Where could the light be coming from? Should I open the door?*

After debating with himself for a full thirty seconds, Jeremy flung the door open, not sure what he expected to find. To his surprise, the room was completely dark.

Jeremy scratched his head in bewilderment. *I know I saw a light. Didn't I?* Jeremy's mind raced as he tiptoed into the nursery to check on the twins. He cautiously glanced around the room for anything that might be out of place. Jeremy spread Matthew's blue blanket over the boy's small legs. Finding Morgan's stuffed elephant had fallen through the slats of her crib, he set the animal on the mattress at her feet. Satisfied that the babies were okay, Jeremy stepped into the dark hallway and closed the door behind him. He leaned back against the wall opposite the door and held his breath as he waited for the light to reappear.

Engulfed in darkness, the only sound Jeremy heard came from the clock at the far end of the hallway as the hands ticked away the night. He realized he was holding his breath, and slowly let the air out through his lips. Convinced that the light wasn't going to reappear, Jeremy shook his head and continued down the hall toward the bathroom.

*

Two nights later, Jeremy and Michelle were cuddled on the couch watching the last episode of a new television series called *Celebrity Ghost Stories*. The twins were in bed, and Jeremy was thankful for a few minutes alone with his wife. He buried his nose in his wife's hair and breathed deeply.

"I will never understand how you take care of two eleven-month-olds and still manage to smell so good," Jeremy whispered in Michelle's ear.

Michelle laughed and nudged him in the ribs with her elbow. "Stop that. You do just as much with them as I do."

Jeremy shook his head but was too tired to argue. Instead, he turned his attention to the television and watched as actor Anson Williams, who played Potsie on *Happy Days*, shared the story of his paranormal encounter.

When the episode ended, Jeremy sat up and exclaimed, "That has to be it." His voice woke his dozing wife.

"What? What has to be it?" Michelle asked as she rubbed her eyes and looked at her husband, her left eyebrow raised in confusion.

"Potsie's story!" Jeremy cried. When his wife just stared at him, Jeremy said, "You weren't watching, were you?"

Michelle smiled and bit her lip, her eyelids drooping. "I might have been resting my eyes a little." She winked and continued, "But tell me about it. I want to hear what has you so excited."

"Do you remember how I told you I saw a flickering, golden light reflecting on the floor outside the twins' room the other night?" Jeremy asked.

Michelle nodded but said nothing.

"I'll admit, I didn't know what to make of it. On the one hand it scared me, made me wonder if I had seen a ghost, but it warmed my heart at the same time," Jeremy said.

"Okay, but what does that have to do with the show?" Michelle asked.

"I'm getting to that part," Jeremy said, bopping his wife playfully on the nose. "Anson Williams was telling his ghost story. Apparently he was born right after his grandmother died, so he never got to meet her. One night when his parents opened his nursery door to check on him, they saw a golden light and the bust of his grandmother looking over the side of the crib."

Michelle smiled. "I can take it from here," she said, pecking Jeremy on the cheek. "You think the light you saw was your mom checking in on her grandchildren."

Jeremy shrugged, a grin plastered across his face. "I don't know that it was, but I certainly don't know that it wasn't either," he paused. "I do know that I don't believe in ghosts. But honestly? Nothing would make me happier than to know that Mom got to meet them."

Michelle smiled and laid her head on Jeremy's chest. "Me, neither, Jeremy. Me, neither."

*

Jeremy sat at the computer in the living room, checking the game recaps from the March Madness basketball games he had fallen asleep during the night before. From his chair, he could see Michelle cooking dinner in the kitchen. Her hair was pulled up in a messy bun, and a floral apron protected her jeans and pink sweater from stains.

"Jeremy?" Michelle called, not bothering to look up from the dough she was kneading. A baby monitor sat on the edge of the counter.

"Yes, dear?" he replied.

"Morgan is crying," she said, motioning to the monitor with her head. "Would you grab her before she wakes her brother up, too?"

Jeremy closed the window he was using, stood, and pushed the computer chair under the desk. "I'm on it," he said.

Michelle smiled. "Thanks, sweetheart."

Jeremy dashed into the kitchen and planted a kiss on her cheek. "Anything for you, my dear." As he headed for the nursery, he called back, "By the way, I like the pale look. The flour really does something for your complexion."

Michelle laughed as Jeremy walked down the hallway toward the nursery. He paused with his hand on the brass doorknob, remembering the countless times over the past seven months that he'd glimpsed the faint golden glow peeking out from underneath the door and the familiar warmth that would flood his body as he imagined his mother checking on her grandchildren.

Jeremy pushed the door open and saw Morgan standing by the railing of her crib. Her face was wet with a mixture of tears and snot. The twins were already eighteen months old and getting into everything. It was only a matter of time before they figured out how to escape the confines of their cribs.

"Well hello there, pretty girl," Jeremy cooed as he picked up his daughter and placed her on his hip. He grabbed a tissue from the nightstand and wiped her nose and eyes. "Shh, it's okay. Daddy's here," he whispered.

Jeremy peeked over the edge of Matthew's crib. The boy was sound asleep with his thumb in his mouth. Jeremy smiled and carried Morgan toward the nursery door.

When they were safely in the hall, Jeremy switched Morgan to his other hip. The toddler laid her head on his shoulder as he scratched her back. Family portraits lined the hallway, and Jeremy held Morgan while she studied the faces in a picture of his mother, his two siblings, and him.

Morgan pointed at the picture, and Jeremy moved closer so that she could touch the faces. The toddler placed her chubby finger on his mother's face and said, "Granny Beth."

Jeremy looked at his daughter, shocked and surprised. He had never told either of the twins about his mother. They weren't old enough to understand. There was no way Morgan could've known who the woman in the picture was, unless...

Jeremy smiled and kissed his daughter on the top of the head. "That's exactly right, sweetheart. That's Granny Beth. She loves you very much."

Epilogue

Romans 8:28 – And we know that in all things God works for the good of those who love Him, who have been called according to his purpose.

    Truth be told, the writing of this book has been one of the greatest God Moments of my life for two reasons.
    First, because of the financial situation of my family, the responsibility to fund my graduate education was to fall on my shoulders. I told God I really didn't want to go into debt chasing my crazy "write a book dream," but after my acceptance to the Professional Writing

program at the University of Oklahoma, the days flew by without the offer of an assistantship.

Believing that the University of Oklahoma was where I was supposed to be, I told them I was coming and waited to see how the future would play out. Less than two weeks before I was to start the drive out to Oklahoma, I received an email offering me a graduate assistantship to the university. Tuition waved, monthly stipend, both mine for the taking. That was my fleece on the ground, the neon sign I was looking for, the confirmation that I was on the right path.

I second-guess myself and my decisions a lot, even when things are going well. Thankfully, my God comes along and reminds me that I don't have to understand, I am only asked to trust and obey. My reminder of this fact came less than a year after my move to Oklahoma, when I approached a professor at the university about being part of the committee for my book defense. I was nervous because while I knew exactly the book I had in mind to write for my Final Project, I was also aware of the fact that I was a student in a prestigious writing program, where genre, market-based fiction writing was encouraged, a style completely opposite of the book I intended to write. I was so apprehensive, in fact, that I came up with another idea to present as a Plan A, leaving my real idea cautiously on the backburner as a second idea. I approached the meeting cautiously and shared both ideas with my professor, and to my surprise, he said these words, "I'd choose the second one. I think there's a market for that. I think it'll sell."

Those words were the green light to begin the process for what you now hold in your hand. While I still faced the challenge of incorporating biblical truths with the conventions and best practices of nonfiction and short story writing, my professors were supportive, and my God proved faithful time and time again.

I hope that through the pages of this book and the truths intertwined in each and every story, you have seen the incredible ways God has worked miracles in my life and the lives of my friends. I pray that even now you have begun to glimpse His mysterious hand working in yours. And my desire is that you start to notice and to treasure the God Moments – the little miracles of grace – that He chooses to lavish on you, just because He can.

Acknowledgements

Philippians 1:3,8 – I thank my God every time I remember you. God can testify how I long for all of you with the affection of Christ Jesus.

    There are so many people that need to be thanked – for their support, for their stories, for their strength, for their love. These people stood with me through the teary phone calls, stressful deadlines, and little victories along the way.

    Mom and Dad. Without your support and encouragement, I wouldn't have had the courage to take on the adventure of grad school so far from home. The daily texts we exchanged, Mom, made me feel a little less lonely and like home wasn't quite so far away. Dad, the flights you financed so that I could actually experience home for a long weekend, kept me energized and motivated, believing my task was doable. You both were witnesses to just about every one of these stories so I'm grateful for the opportunity to have shared these moments with you not once, but twice.

My brothers, Greg and Andrew. The ridiculous texts, Snapchats, and tweets you sent me over the past two years never failed to make me smile or reminded me how great it is to have a family that cares for each other. Like Mom and Dad, you both saw some of these moments first-hand, so I pray that you remember how big your God really is and that He is always fighting on your behalf.

My grandparents, Mama & Papa, Nana & Poppa. Throughout my life, you have always been my biggest cheerleaders. I was blessed with living five minutes away from all of you – something that most grandkids will never be able to state as truth. You taught me what love is. Your actions showed me that it's possible to love the same someone for a very long time and that God's love has no conditions. You never missed an opportunity to express your love for me. I wish you could all see first-hand the fruit of your love in this book.

Kristi. I prayed for a sister and God gave me you. Your friendship over the past eight years has been life-changing. I mean that. Thank you for always believing in me and my stories and for just the right balance of sympathy on the really bad days and tough love on the days when I'm ready to give up. I couldn't have completed this journey without you. My desire is that you never forget to look for the little ways God loves on you every single day.

My committee members and professors, both in Oklahoma and South Carolina. You not only taught me many things about writing but also about accepting a challenge and facing it head on. You've made me a better teacher, learner, and writer. I'm grateful for your patience and guidance. I hope that I'm able to make you proud and that you've been blessed even a little by seeing the great things my God can do.

My roommates, Brandy, Abigail, and Sarah. It's hard not to write when you're constantly being asked how much you accomplished each day. You kept me on task, on deadline, and kept me laughing all the way. You'll never know how much that meant. The grace of God to give me you three as roommates is proof that He really does have our best interest at heart, that He knows exactly what He's doing. You are a true gift.

My friends and family. Thank you for your stories, for sharing your lives with me. Every time I came home, you asked me how the book was coming along or when you would be able to read it. Well, here it is. I hope you enjoyed it. I pray that you don't stop with just reading my stories, but that you look for the hand of God working in your lives each and every day. I love His promise in Isaiah 43:18 – "But forget all that – it is nothing compared to what I am going to do." Be on the lookout for those things He is just waiting to do for you!

And last, but not least, my ever-faithful God. You gave me this idea; You gave me these stories. I pray that You are pleased with my efforts and that You alone receive the glory for these words.

About the Author

Lauren Stephens is a native of Aiken, South Carolina. She graduated from the University of Oklahoma in May 2015 with a Master's of Professional Writing. Before pursuing her writing career in Norman, Oklahoma, Lauren attended the University of South Carolina Aiken, where she received her Bachelor's degree in Secondary Education Mathematics in 2011 and spent the next year and a half teaching math and English at the high school level. She will begin the journey toward her Doctorate in August 2015 at Clemson University.

Lauren has written an interdisciplinary middle school curriculum that is published in print and online. She traveled throughout the country presenting the research and education techniques involved in this curriculum and was published in the 2012 South Carolina Middle School Journal. The curriculum is available at http://www.drmclient.com/edgewood/.

In her spare time, Lauren enjoys running marathons, binge-watching college football and basketball, and consuming all the milkshakes and Chick-fil-a she can get her hands on.

You can connect with Lauren on Facebook and Twitter:
facebook.com/WallyBeth
twitter.com/wallywithwords

Made in the USA
San Bernardino, CA
27 June 2015